Fun Things To Do With My Granddaughter

Ideas for Meaningful Times Together

Spending time with our granddaughters is always precious. But why settle for simply spending time together when we can invest in it? Let's invest in a deeper relationship, one that grows stronger and closer as the years go by. The first step is being more intentional about the moments we share. This book holds hundreds of ideas to help you do just that. With a little thought, a lot of love, and a few materials you're likely to have on hand, today is the perfect time to start investing in a more beautiful, meaningful tomorrow, shared with those who matter most.

These projects are recommended for children 8 and above. Grandparents, always carefully supervise your grandchildren when enjoying these activities together, especially around water, in the kitchen, or when using sharp objects. Remember that any activity involving small parts can present a choking hazard and is not suitable for children under the age of 3. Before beginning any activity, take into consideration your grandchildren's ages, abilities, and any allergies they may have, and adapt your plans accordingly. Stay safe and have fun!

Fun Things To Do With My Granddaughter
ISBN 978-1-7350245-7-8
Published by Product Concept Mfg., Inc., 2175 N. Academy Circle #7, Colorado Springs, CO 80909
©2021 Product Concept Mfg., Inc. All rights reserved.
Written and Compiled by Vicki Kuyper in association with Product Concept Mfg., Inc.

GRANDDAUGHTER'S CHOICE

As a grandmother, it's easy to slide into the rut of "running the show" when our granddaughter comes to visit. But as our granddaughters mature, they need less direction from us and more room to express their own individual tastes and abilities. Every granddaughter, and grandmother, is unique. We may love cooking, crafts, and "girly" décor. Our granddaughters may enjoy sports, dinosaurs, and animation. Or vice versa. Our job is to help our granddaughters grow into the women they were born to be—not who we wish they were, or who we wish we had grown up to be. Grandparenting is an opportunity for growth on both ends of the relationship. With love, forethought, and a little creativity, we can use the time we have together in memorable, enjoyable, positive ways.

One way to do that is to schedule a Granddaughter's Choice Day. Allow your granddaughter the opportunity to choose the activities and menu for her visit. If something she suggests isn't possible, explain why, and help her come up with a workable alternative.

READY, SET...SWITCH!

A fun—and revealing—game to play with your granddaughter is spending five or ten minutes imitating each other. Ask her to be the grandmother, while you be the granddaughter. Try to get her speech patterns and mannerisms down, but always in a flattering way. Pay attention to how she imitates you. Is there anything you feel you'd like to change about the way she sees you? Don't take the game too personally. Use it as an opportunity to see yourself as others might see you.

"GETTÏNG TO KNOW YOU" FÏLE

Every visit with your granddaughter is an opportunity to get to know her better. Listen carefully when she talks to you. Ask questions. Who's her best friend? What makes her such a good friend? Find out what foods she likes—and can't stand. What's her favorite movie? Band? Video game? How would she describe her "perfect day"? What makes her sad? What's she afraid of? What does she like best about herself?

Don't make her feel as though she's the subject of an interrogation. You don't need to know every detail of her life in one visit. Just take your conversations to a deeper level, in a way that feels natural. If you're truly interested in getting to know her better, it will show.

After your visit, take a few moments to jot down what you've learned about your granddaughter in a journal or on a 3 x 5 card. Before her next visit, review what you've written. Then, you can ask your granddaughter how her best friend is doing by name or serve her a lunch that features her favorite food.

Pay attention when her preferences change and inquire in a non-invasive way as to why. Recognize that maturing is a roller-coaster process. Her moods and attitudes toward you and others will have their ups and downs as time goes by. But if your granddaughter knows you are a safe person and your home is a safe place where she can honestly be herself—and that you will love her no matter what—your relationship will continue to deepen and mature right along with her.

REFASHION THE FAMILY JEWELS

Look through your jewelry box with your granddaughter, telling her stories about how you acquired the pieces you own and the special places that you've worn them. Then, either pass one piece down to her to keep OR take pieces you no longer use and work together to fashion them into something your granddaughter would enjoy wearing. Try making a bracelet out of the beads from an old necklace by restringing them on a piece of elastic. Using fabric glue, bedazzle your granddaughter's jeans with rhinestones from a brooch or pendant. Take the dangling décor from a pair of earrings and hang it from a safety pin that can be fastened on a backpack or jean jacket. Get creative and help your granddaughter begin her own jewelry box filled with the most precious of gems, treasured memories.

GRANDMA & GRANDDAUGHTER BOOK CLUB

Book clubs aren't just for grown-ups. Start a very special one, just between your granddaughter and you. Together, choose a mix of classics, personal favorites that you read when you were young, books on the current bestseller list geared toward her age, as well as any of her favorite books that she would like to share with you. Read them together, or separately, depending on how frequently you are able to spend time together. Then, set up a special time to talk about what you've read, discussing what you enjoyed, what you didn't, and why.

invisible Love notes

Everyone appreciates a hand-written note of encouragement, appreciation, or affirmation. Take a twist on an old classic by writing your granddaughter "secret" messages for her to find and decipher. Prepare the notes before she arrives, hiding them around your home. Draw a little heart in red marker on the corner of the note so she knows this isn't just a random piece of "blank" paper laying around. To write your note, mix lemon juice with a little bit of water to use as your "ink." Use a cotton swab for your "pen." Print clearly and keep your message simple, using just a few words. Once your granddaughter has gathered the hidden notes, show her how to hold them over a warm light bulb briefly. The heat will make your little words of love appear!

LEARN SOMETHING NEW

You CAN teach an old grandma new tricks! And sometimes, it's your granddaughter who will be the teacher. Ask your granddaughter what she's learned lately. Then, ask her to teach you. It may be how to play a musical instrument, master a soccer move, or make it to the next level on her favorite video game. Be a willing and attentive student. Ask questions. Compliment her on her newly acquired skill or knowledge. Everyone, regardless of his or her age, has something to teach and something left to learn!

MAiL CALL

Ask your granddaughter if she's ever felt lonely and, if so, what made her feel that way. Then talk about what would have made her feel less alone. Ask if she can think of anyone who might feel lonely right now. Add anyone you can think of, particularly relatives your granddaughter would know. Then work together to bring a little bit of love and friendship into the lives of those you just mentioned. Write a letter or make a homemade card and send it on its way today.

COMICAL CHARACTERS

Work together with your granddaughter to make a comic strip starring you and her! Come up with a name, a silly storyline, and easily-drawn images of your two main characters. Have your grand-daughter be responsible for drawing you and you draw her. Who knows? Your comic strip might become so popular that it runs for years!

MOViE CRiTiCS

When you and your granddaughter watch movies together, don't let the opportunity pass you by to use it as an invitation to get to know each other better. Spend a few minutes afterwards talking about the pros and cons of the story. How are you alike, or different, from the characters? Would you have made the same choices? What was the message of the movie? Do you agree or disagree with it? Is there any part of the story you would have liked to have turned out a different way? Is it worth watching again?

PRIVATE CODED MESSAGES

Although what you and your granddaughter have to tell each other isn't necessarily a secret, it's fun to share a language that only you and she can understand. Decide what you will use as your code. For instance, use the third letter that comes after the letter you actually want to write. Instead of A, write D. If you want to write Z, circle back to the beginning of the alphabet and write C. Or, try a book cipher. Use a book that both of you have on hand, such as the same translation of the Bible or one of the books that you choose to read together for your book club. It is important that you both have a copy of the very same edition. Then, find the word you want to use in the pages of the book. Write the page number, number of lines from the top of the page, and number of words in from the left where your chosen word is found. So your clue for each word would read something like this: 30-4-15. That means your chosen word is on page 30, the fourth line from the top and the 15th word from the left. Use your special code to write messages to each other when you're together and to write letters to each other when you're apart!

AL-PHOTO-BET SEARCH

Go on an Al-PHOTO-bet walk through the neighborhood with your granddaughter, looking for things that begin with different letters of the alphabet. Either take photos of objects that begin with every letter of the alphabet or choose one letter and only take photos of objects that begin with that letter. If your granddaughter has a younger sibling or cousin, work together to use these photos to make him or her an Alphabet Photo Book. You can either print the photos and put them in an album or tape them to sheets of paper stapled together to make a book or go online and download them to make a hardcover photo book that will last for years.

THEN AND NOW

Use time driving together in the car or waiting in line to play a game that helps you and your granddaughter learn more about each other. Play Then and Now. Compare how things were done when you were your granddaughter's age with how she does things now. For instance, talk about how you researched papers for school, using the library and encyclopedias, instead of the internet. Or share how you had to save up money to call a friend long distance and how you had to actually remember someone's phone number to call her—by turning a rotary dial.

WE COULD USE THAT!

Any time you or your granddaughter find a task or situation difficult, brainstorm together about an invention that could make that particular task easier. Have fun with your idea by coming up with a catchy name and slogan to sell your new invention. Then make an advertisement by drawing a poster or making a video on your phone selling your idea to the world.

WHO WORE IT WORST?

Look at your granddaughter's baby book, family photo albums, and your old school yearbooks. Together, vote for the craziest hairstyle, wackiest outfit, and funniest photo of the bunch.

TIMELESS LIFE HACKS

Since homemaking skills are rarely taught in school, why not pick up the teaching mantle and help your granddaughter master a few life hacks that have stood the test of time? Better yet, why not have some fun doing it? Here are a few ideas to get you started:

BUTTONIZE IT!

Sewing on a button isn't rocket science, but loose or lost buttons are usually considered a Mom Job. Give Mom a break by showing your granddaughter how much fun you can have with a needle and thread. Show your granddaughter how to thread a needle and tie a knot in the end of the thread. Then, dig up any odd buttons you have laying around, whether they're from your sewing box or are the extra buttons often included when you purchase clothing. You can also pick up a variety of fun sale buttons the next time you're at a hobby store to keep on hand.

Have your granddaughter help you replace a set of boring buttons on a button-down shirt with a variety of different ones, the funkier and more colorful, the better. Have your granddaughter bring along a jean jacket and sew button designs on the pockets. It's easy to make flowers with button petals or a funny face with button eyes and a smile. Get creative.

PATCH IT UP

Help your granddaughter patch up any holes in her jeans (at least the ones that aren't there for the sake of fashion!) with iron-on patches. Cut the store-bought patches into fun shapes, such as hearts or flowers, before ironing them on. Or have your granddaughter paint them with child-safe fabric paint after they've been ironed on.

Giggles 'n' Grins

Knock-Knock
Who's there?
Ella!
Ella who?
Ella-vator, and I'm here to
give you a lift!

Knock-Knock
Who's there?
Noise!
Noise who?
Noise to see you!

Knock-Knock
Who's there?
Owl.
Owl who?
Owl be sad if you don't
open the door!

Knock-Knock
Who's there?
Wire.
Wire who?
Wire you not opening
the door?

Knock-Knock
Who's there?
Sharon.
Sharon who?
Sharon share alike!

Knock-Knock
Who's there?
Hatch.
Hatch who?
God bless you!

Knock-Knock
Who's there?
Alex.
Alex who?
Alex the questions!

Knock-Knock
Who's there?
Althea.
Althea who?
Althea later, alligator!

Knock-Knock
Who's there?
Doris.
Doris who?
Doris locked, that's
why I had to knock!

GG'S SPA DAY

Invite your granddaughter to enjoy a day of personal pampering at GG's Spa. (That stands for Grandmothers and Granddaughters!) Spa time is not only relaxing, but relational. It offers you a chance to get up close and personal with each other in an atmosphere that invites laughter and natural conversation.

Dress in comfy robes and slippers. Put on soft music in the background. Then, paint each other's nails. Put lotion on each other's hands and feet. Massage each other's shoulders. Have fun fixing each other's hair with barrettes, bobby pins, and clips. Or go a step further by using hair gel, colorful hair chalk, or spray-on hair glitter, color, or highlights (all of which wash out easily).

You may even want to go with the full spa treatment, enjoying homemade facials, giving each other a make-up makeover, and serving light snacks on fancy, festive dishes. Focus on whatever you feel is appropriate for your granddaughter's age and interest. Here are a few homemade concoctions to get your spa day underway...

LOVELY LEMON FOOTSOAK

Fill a small, plastic storage container with warm water, adding 1 to 3 cups of vinegar. Immerse a pair of clean, deserving feet. Cut 1 to 3 lemons in half and squeeze the juice into the water/vinegar mixture. Use the lemon peels to scrub excess skin from your granddaughter's feet. Then, scrub her feet with Epson salt. Add 1 to 3 cups of Epson salts, and more warm water, if needed, to the tub. Soak for 15 to 60 minutes. Put feet in a cool, fresh water bath when done, rubbing them with a clean washcloth to remove any excess dry skin. Then, if she's comfortable, have your granddaughter give you the same treatment!

DIY GLITTER NAILS

For fun, fancy nails, try adding a little sparkle. Put petroleum jelly around your granddaughter's nails to make excess glitter easier to remove. Apply one coat of nail polish, either clear or colored. Immediately, shake glitter on top of wet nails. Tap excess glitter off onto a sheet of paper. Once the nails are dry, cover with two coats of clear polish to help seal in the glitter. For extra fun, use heart or flower-shaped glitter. Or, paint nails with colored nail polish, and then put large dots of clear polish on top of the dry nails, using a toothpick. Shake on some glitter. When you shake off the excess glitter, your granddaughter's nails will be sporting sparkling polka-dots.

INVIGORATING FACIAL

Use an elastic headband to hold your hair back from your face. Mix up a quick and easy facial by whisking together 1 tsp. of honey, 1 tsp. of milk, and 1 tsp. of mashed avocado. Leave the mixture on your face for 20 to 30 minutes and then rinse off with warm water. Put a slice of cucumber on your eyes while you wait, for the true spa experience.

REFRESHING SPA BEVERAGES

Make fancy flavored-water, spa-style, by adding strawberries and slices of lemon or sliced cucumber and mint leaves to a pitcher of cold water. Allow it to sit in the fridge for at least 1 hour before serving. Or make Italian sodas by mixing sparkling water with a few tablespoons of flavored beverage syrups and serve over ice. To enjoy a little decadence, add a splash of cream or half and half to make an Italian cream soda.

Don't forget to take a few photos during your pampering time together, so you can look back on all of the fun you had.

SLUMBER PARTY FUN

IT'S IN THE STARS!

The next time your granddaughter spends the night at your house, do a little stargazing—inside! Draw a fairly simple picture on a sheet of construction paper. Use a large safety pin to poke holes around the edges of the drawing, about ¼ inch apart. Then, turn off the lights and shine a flashlight behind the paper. Poof—instant starry night! Be sure and give your new constellation a heavenly name.

WRITE-YOUR-OWN BEDTIME STORY

Instead of reading a story before bedtime, write your own. Let your granddaughter come up with the first line. Then you add the next line, and so on, back and forth. If you like, set a timer for five minutes. When it goes off, you each get to add one more line to finish it off.

SUPER GRANDMA

Before you tuck your granddaughter in for the night, show her you're a Super Grandma. Have her sit on the edge of the bed and put your finger on her forehead. Then ask her to stand up without using her hands. She can't! That's because to rise from a sitting position to standing, we need to lean forward. Even a small bit of pressure has the power to keep us in place.

NURTURE AN ATTITUDE OF GRATITUDE

When you sit down to share a meal with your granddaughter, nurture an attitude of gratitude. If you usually say grace together before meals, incorporate three things you are grateful for into your prayer, and encourage your granddaughter to do the same. You can also write three things you're each thankful for on slips of paper. Share your reasons for thanks aloud and then put them into a jar that you use as a centerpiece on the table. Try and come up with different reasons for gratitude at each meal. As you watch the jar fill up, you'll both be reminded of how much you have to be thankful for.

"I'M THANKFUL FOR..." PHOTO CHALLENGE

Developing an attitude of gratitude has been shown to boost a more positive outlook on life, while reducing stress and negativity. Helping your granddaughter (and yourself!) greet each day with a more thankful heart can be a life-changing gift to each other. To become more aware of the countless blessings each new day brings your way, try this fun photo challenge. All you'll need is an easy-to-operate camera or camera phone. Come up with a theme for the day, such as family, friendship, nourishment, nature, beauty, comfort, health, safety, amusement, wonder, or love. Then, see how many things you can capture photographically in one day that illustrate how this theme is evident in your life. You can do this activity together, or if your granddaughter has access to her own phone at home, challenge her to text you at least one photo each day that captures something she's thankful for. You can print the photos and make an annual "Things I'm Thankful for This Year" book or simply talk about the photos you take. Either way, you'll both find yourselves becoming more aware of the many reasons to say "thanks" throughout the day.

THEME DAYS

Turn an ordinary day into a memorable celebration by focusing on a specific theme. Here are a few ideas to get your creative juices flowing:

- Work with your granddaughter to come up with an alliterative or rhyming theme for each day of the week. For instance, Sunday might be Fun Day, when you play board games together. Tuesday is No Shoes Day, the perfect time for pedicures or for only wearing slippers. Or how about Thirsty Thursdays, when you celebrate with root beer floats?

- Everyone enjoys the occasional Pajama Day. Celebrate with movies, hot cocoa, and flannel.

- Grandma For a Day invites your granddaughter to raid your closet and dress up like you. Give her the opportunity to choose a grandmotherly nickname you can refer to her throughout the day. Nana, GiGi, The Grandster...what moniker suits her best?

- Inside-Out Day is time to turn conventional fashion on its head. Wear your clothes inside out.

- Pick a color and make it a day-long theme. Make sure your outfit and food choices meet the colorful criteria. You may want to offer little surprise gifts if your granddaughter can figure out how to work the name of the color into your conversation. For instance, you can talk about what it means to feel "in the pink," or "green with envy," or to find your piggy bank is "in the red."

- Have a No Silverware meal—and don't play it safe with a sandwich. Serve up macaroni and cheese or yogurt. Finish it off with a long bubble bath!

TREASURED TV MOMENTS

Make the most of the time you spend in front of the television with your granddaughter by using it not only as a relaxing pastime, but a relational teaching tool. Recall your favorite television shows and movies when you were your granddaughter's age. Most of them are undoubtedly available on DVD or through a streaming service. Choose a favorite that you think your granddaughter would enjoy and watch it together. (You may even want to have your favorite childhood snack on hand for you two to munch on!) Talk about what was different (such as having your home phone connected to the wall) and what remains the same (such as how families love each other). Discuss why you have such fond memories of the show. Ask your granddaughter to review what you watched. The next time you get together, have your granddaughter choose a movie or TV show that she loves and watch it together. Share your review of what you watched with her.

GOOD OLD DAYS GAME TIME

Childhood games may go in and out of style, but it doesn't mean they are any less fun to play now than they were way back when. What did you do to pass the time when you were your granddaughter's age? Play with jacks? Card games? Jump rope? Did you make paper dolls out of department store catalog pages—or chew wintergreen candy in a darkened room with friends, so you could watch the sparks fly? Introduce your granddaughter to a few nostalgic pastimes that may become some of her new favorites.

"GETTING TO KNOW YOU" SCAVENGER HUNT

Instead of hiding a treasure, allow your granddaughter to use her "relational intelligence" to gather the items needed to earn a special treat. Give her a list of items she needs to collect around your home and a basket or bag to collect them in.

The key is to give your granddaughter clues that relate to you or her. Let her know that she's allowed to ask you questions along the way, anytime she needs help. This game is designed so that she will need your help along the way, and you will get to know each other a little better at the same time. Be sure and show your granddaughter where she's allowed to search and anywhere that is "off limits." Once she finds all of the items on the list, award her with a small, wrapped gift—or treat her to an ice cream run.

Here are examples of clues you can use to help her gather items that reveal a bit about you:

Bring me something that is my favorite color.

Bring me something that is YOUR favorite color.

Bring me one of my favorite snacks.

Bring me something I like to do in my spare time.

Bring me something that reminds me of you.

Bring me something that reminds YOU of me!

Bring me a book you'd like to read.

Bring me something of mine you wished you had!
(This may give you a clue for a future Christmas or
birthday gift!)

FIND THAT COLOR!

Have your granddaughter gather something from every color of the rainbow, such as a red apple, a white sock, and a blue pen. You can also do a verbal scavenger hunt anytime you find yourself waiting in line or on a drive together in the car. Choose a color and then see who'll be the first to locate something sporting your chosen hue. Or choose a category, such as fruits or animals. Then, name something in that category that is orange, green, yellow, purple, etc.

PICTURE BOOK SCAVENGER HUNT

For a fun, quiet time activity, gather a stack of picture books and give your granddaughter a list of things to find in them. For instance: Find a cat; Find a teacup; Find the word "love"; Find the color purple; Find the letter Z. Have her write the title of the book and page number beside each object she finds on the list.

TOUCHY-FEELY SCAVENGER SEARCH

For this interactive scavenger hunt, you can either make a list of objects for your granddaughter to search for or you can simply give her a new "assignment" every time she brings a found object back to you. Ask her to find things of different shapes, textures, smells, etc. For instance, ask her to find something shiny, something she can twist, something she can roll, something that smells sweet, something that is clear, something bumpy, something squishy, etc.

XOXO MARKS THE SPOT

   Hide a special XOXO goodie box for your granddaughter by filling a shoebox with tiny treasures, such as candy, barrettes, small toys, costume jewelry, etc. Write clues on index cards and hide them around your home, each clue leading to the next one, and eventually to the box of hidden treasure. Give your granddaughter an envelope she can collect the clues in and lead her to the first clue. Here are a few clue ideas to get your creative juices flowing:

I have a tongue, but I can't tell you where the treasure is! (Leads to a clue that's set inside a shoe in your closet)

I'm in a bowl that you DON'T want to eat your cereal out of! (Leads to a clue taped to a closed toilet seat lid)

I have a sinking feeling you'll find me after you clear off the kitchen table. (Leads to a clue sealed in a plastic bag in the kitchen sink)

I have the power to change what you see! (Leads to a clue taped to the TV remote)

You'll find me where a very special little girl rests her sweet little head. (Leads to a clue inside your granddaughter's pillowcase.)

EGGS-QUISITE WREATH

Work together with your granddaughter to make a wreath for your front door or for the door of her bedroom at home. You'll need a large piece of cardboard, an empty cardboard egg carton, glue, and whatever you'd like to use to decorate your wreath, such as paints, markers, crayons, stickers, or glitter. Use your imagination to cut and decorate the egg cups (and even the dividers!) into flower shapes, animal faces, emojis, Easter eggs, Valentine hearts, Santa faces, autumn leaves, beach umbrellas…anything you can think of that fits the season you're in. Cut a large piece of heavy cardboard into a donut-shape for the base. Decorate your egg cups as you like and then glue them onto the base. After they dry, secure a hook or string at the top of the wreath, so you can hang it from a door or hook on the wall to welcome in guests, as well as the coming season.

WASHER NECKLACES

The next time you clean out your Fix-It box, gather unused washers to make stylish necklaces with your granddaughter. Paint one side of the washer with nail polish, allowing each color to dry before adding another. Loop a length of yarn, twine, or a chain or suede rope from a necklace you no longer use, and push it through the middle opening of the washer. Pull the rest of the yarn through the loop to secure it to the washer. Make sure the yarn is long enough to easily fit over your head. If you like, thread a few beads onto the yarn before tying the ends together.

LAZY DAY CRAZY MAZE

If you and your granddaughter are stuck inside due to inclement weather, burn off a little excess energy by making a Lazy Day Crazy Maze. Tape crepe paper or string to the walls of a hallway in a zigzag design, going high and low. Then, challenge your granddaughter to make her way through the maze without touching any of the "laser" beams by stepping over or crawling under them. Make the maze even more challenging by taping plastic flowers or disposable plastic lids on the wall throughout the maze that your granddaughter has to collect as she makes her way through. If your granddaughter's a flexibility pro, clip bobby pins or barrettes on the crepe paper and challenge her to remove each of them without having any of the maze pull away from the wall. Time her to see if she can beat her own time!

If you really want to bond with her, you have to do more than build the maze and watch. You'll need to participate! Tell her you'll go through the maze once she's made it through without a hitch. Even if you don't make it very far, you and your granddaughter are sure to share a good laugh over your attempt!

THE imAGiNATiON STATiON

Never run out of good ideas for how to spend time together by enlisting your granddaughter in making an Imagination Station jar. Work together to brainstorm ideas of things you'd like to do together…activities, crafts, outings, conversational topics, etc. Ideas can include things like, "Play 20 Questions," "Go for a walk around the block," "Read a book," or "Make a card to send to a friend." Write each idea on a separate piece of paper and put it into a jar. Have your granddaughter pull a slip of paper out of the jar anytime you could both use a little added inspiration.

NEIGHBORHOOD CRAFT SALE

Every child looks forward to a little extra spending money. Instead of giving your granddaughter gifts of cash, help her earn it in an enjoyable way. Work on some of the projects in this book with the intent of selling them. Discuss what is a reasonable price and what items people are most willing to buy. See if there is a local church or school craft sale, or farmers' market, she can participate in, or offer her creations on a separate table when it's time for a garage sale. It will help your granddaughter put her math skills to practical use and learn a bit about pricing, display, advertising, and the costs that are sometimes involved in making money. Who knows? It could become an annual event you both can share.

ROCK ON

An easy, inexpensive project to work on with your granddaughter is turning rocks into works of art. Whether the rocks come from your garden, or you take a walk together to gather them, talk about the best way to decorate them. Perhaps the shape of the rock suggests an animal you'd like to paint on it. Or maybe you'd like to paint a short word of encouragement or inspiration on each rock. Paint them with nail polish or acrylic paints. (Remember, acrylic paints are not washable, so cover clothing and work surfaces when working with it.) There are even markers specifically designed to write on rocks or glass. Then, figure out what the finished rocks should be used for: to decorate your yard, to display on your granddaughter's dresser at home, to give as gifts to friends, to leave along the trail of a local park...

TWIRLING TRIANGLES JEWELRY

Whether you're helping your granddaughter make gifts for family, friends, or herself, doing crafts together that involves repetitive movements invites casual conversation. Here's a perfect activity that can be easily mastered, allowing plenty of time to chat while you create something beautiful at the same time.

You'll need scissors, old magazines, glue, a sewing or darning needle with a large eye, and yarn, twine, or plastic thread. Cut triangles, about 12 inches long and 1½" wide at the bottom, out of colorful magazine pages. You can vary the size of the triangles to add a bit of variety to your necklace by making your paper "beads" differ in size. Thread the needle with the yarn or cord you wish to use as the base strand of your necklace. Make sure that when it's tied it will easily fit over your head (or your granddaughter's) with a few inches to spare. Put a large knot in one end, leaving at least an inch beyond it to tie to the other end when your necklace is complete.

Wrap one of the triangles tightly around the needle, starting with the wide end of the paper. When you've finished wrapping the entire triangle, glue the pointed end to hold the wound bead in place. Push it off the needle and down to the knotted end of your yarn or cord. Repeat. You can add pre-made beads, buttons, or even dry, tubular pasta in between your twirling triangle beads. When you've almost filled the string, loosely tie the unknotted end to a coat hanger. Coat all of the paper beads with clear nail polish and let hang until dry. Tie the ends together to finish your eye-catching necklace.

TERRA COTTA TREASURES

At the end of the summer season, pick up some small terra cotta pots. When your granddaughter comes for a visit, decorate them with acrylic paints. (Remember, acrylic paints are not washable, so cover clothing and work surfaces when working with it.) Add some soil and plant seeds or partially sprouted plants. Then, see how much they grow in between visits. If your visits are infrequent, text your granddaughter pictures of your shared plant as it grows!

PERSONALIZED PLACEMATS

Whether you use them for a holiday celebration, or simply to celebrate the gift of spending time with each other, work with your granddaughter to make your own personalized placemats. Decorate pieces of posterboard any way you like. Then, take them to a mail center or office supply store and have them laminated so you can wipe them clean after use. Set them out every time your granddaughter comes for a visit. They are one small way to demonstrate to your granddaughter how keenly you anticipate spending time with her.

EMOJI TALES

Write a story, using only emojis. You and your granddaughter can do this on your phone while you're waiting in line or you can draw your own emojis on a piece of paper at home. After you finish your emoji storyline, tell each other the story the emojis are illustrating.

PHOTO MATCH

Here is a great way to turn a box of old photos into a fun game that will take you on a walk down memory lane. Use a stack of old photos like a deck of cards. (If you haven't thrown out your "reject" photos, they work great!) Deal out 10 cards to each player, photo side down. Then, turn one photo over from the remaining pile to use as the first "inspiration card." The first player places a photo on top of it that matches. It could match in color, the people featured in it, the place it's taken, similar shapes or themes, or how the two images fit together, like a photo of a key and one of a lock. The next person has to match the photo that is now on top of the pile. Chat about the photos as you play. The game ends when you run out of photos or are ready to move on to a different pastime. You and your granddaughter both win because you spent time together!

HiDDEN FiGURES

For this game, all you need are paper plates and sticky notes. The more plates you use, the more difficult the game becomes. Write numbers on as many sticky notes as you have plates—two of each number, to form a match. Then, stick the numbers on the top of the plates, turn them over, and move the plates around, so no one knows where the numbers are. Take turns turning over two plates and trying to make a match. When you succeed, you keep the two plates. The one with the most plates wins. Increase the number of plates you use with every round.

THE GIFT OF A BOOK

Helping your granddaughter nurture a love of reading is a gift she can enjoy for the rest of her life. Once again, think back to the books you enjoyed reading when you were her age. Choose one to read together. If you live far apart, why not send her a copy of one of your favorite childhood books? Set a schedule to read the same chapters at the same time and then chat about what you've read over the phone. For a very special gift, you may want to pass down a book you may have saved from your own childhood to her. Be sure and write something on the dedication page, such as "From the little girl in me who loved this book to the beautiful young woman in you who I hope grows to love it as much as I do."

GG COAT OF ARMS

The special bond between grandmother and granddaughter is worthy of a little extra recognition. Honor that bond in a visible way by making a GG (Grandma/Granddaughter) Coat of Arms that combines symbols that are unique to you and your relationship. For instance, if you share the same last name, incorporate that into your coat of arms. If gathering shells is a favorite shared pastime, add a shell. Perhaps you'll want to list the number of miles that separate your homes or your favorite colors.

Brainstorm what you'd like to include, then look at examples on the internet for more inspiration, and to help you choose the shape of your crest. Cut posterboard into your chosen shape and decorate together. You may want to make two, so you can each have one to display.

GARAGE SALE GALAVANTING

Help your granddaughter gain a passion for recycling, repurposing, and living within her budget by giving her a small amount of cash—and a goal. Then, head out to a garage sale, antique shop, or thrift store. Either work together, or compete against each other, to find a specific item. It could be the funniest, the oldest, the oddest, the best bargain, the best gift for a family member...whatever category fits your mood or your need.

DANCE PARTY CHALLENGE

Get your heart rate, as well as your feet, moving with a grandmother vs. granddaughter dance challenge. Each of you take turns building a dance routine, one step at a time. For instance, you start off with a kick of your right foot. Then, your granddaughter repeats your right foot kick and takes one step to the left. Each of you keep repeating the routine, adding one new step of your own, until one person makes a misstep. You can make it even more difficult by adding an arm motion along with each step!

BACKYARD MINI GOLF

Create your own mini-golf course in your own backyard. Use plastic cups, tin cans with both ends of the can removed, cardboard boxes, rocks, garden gnomes...any type of hole, tunnel, or obstacle your imagination can come up with! If you don't have a golf ball, use a small rubber ball, ping pong ball, or tennis ball. Brooms, plastic baseball bats, or even cardboard paper towel tubes can serve as golf clubs. Since you and your granddaughter made the course, you make up the rules!

PORCH SITTERS

Decorate your home with Grandmother and Granddaughter porch sitters made out of paper bags. Draw your face (and have your granddaughter draw hers) on a paper bag. Keep the features simple outlines, like a jack o' lantern, so you can cut them out. Add yarn or construction paper hair. Cut a pair of legs (wearing your favorite choice of shoes, of course!) and attach them to the front of the bottom of the bag. Put sand, dried beans, rice, or a beanbag, inside the bag to weigh it down. Then, put a glow stick or battery-powered tea light inside. Set your likenesses outside on the porch at sunset, turn on the tea lights, and let your smiles brighten up the neighborhood.

TEA LIGHT LUMINARIAS

Use a variation of your Porch Sitters to decorate for the holidays. Cut a jack o' lantern face, a snowflake, autumn leaf, or Valentine heart-shaped opening out of the front of the bag. Add your weight and a battery-powered tea light to add a festive air to your porch or mantel during the holidays.

FUNNY FACE NIGHTLIGHT

If your granddaughter is spending the night, and could use a little "friend" to help her sleep better in a dark room, have her draw a funny-faced friend on the base of a battery-powered tea light with a permanent marker. Then, have her give her new friend a name—and take him or her to her room as a slumber buddy.

Giggles 'n' Grins

What do you get if you
cross a bunny and a frog?
A bunny ribbit.

What do you get if you
cross a cocker spaniel, a
poodle, and a rooster?
A cockerpoodledoo.

What do you call an
alligator wearing a vest?
An investigator.

What do you call bears
with no ears?
B.

Where do rodents love to
go on vacation?
Hamsterdam.

What snakes are found
on cars?
Windshield vipers.

What keys can't open locks?
Monkeys, donkeys, and turkeys.

What's as big as a
gorilla, but doesn't
weigh anything?
His shadow.

What music do
rabbits like?
Hip hop.

How many tickles does it take to
make an octopus laugh?
Ten-tickles.

Why didn't the turkey
cross the road?
It was too stuffed.

Why did the dog cross
the road?
To get to the barking lot.

What did one flea
say to the other?
Shall we walk, or
take the dog?

Where did the
kittens go on their
school field trip?
To the mew-seum.

PET OWNER PLAYTIME

If your granddaughter could have any kind of pet, what would it be? Feed your granddaughter's imagination, without committing to care for a live animal, by taking a trip to an animal shelter, pet shop, farm, or even the zoo, to view the animal she would love to care for. Talk to those who care for the animals to see what it would actually take to own one. Then, allow your granddaughter to "choose" a pet by taking a picture of it on your phone. On the way home, ask her about her choice. What does she like best about this kind of animal? What would she name it? How would she care for it? What would be hard in terms of caring for it? What would be fun? If the opportunity is available, volunteer with your granddaughter at the zoo or animal shelter to get some hands-on experience.

Here is a cute origami cat you both can do together.

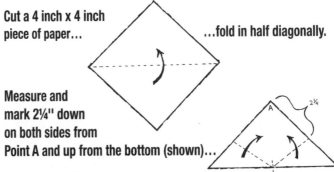

Cut a 4 inch x 4 inch piece of paper…

…fold in half diagonally.

Measure and mark 2¼" down on both sides from Point A and up from the bottom (shown)…

…then fold both outer points in, using marks as guidelines. Fold ¾" down at Point A.

Flip over…   …draw eyes, nose, mouth, and whiskers. Purrr-fect!

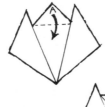

What else can you make by simply folding a piece of paper?

THE AMUSE CRUISE

While setting sail on the seven seas with your granddaughter would be a dream come true, you don't have to break the bank to make happy travel memories together—right where you are. Use a large delivery box as a ship or make a cruise cabin "fort" using furniture, pillows, and blankets.

Look at a map and figure out where you'd like to go. Watch a brief travel video of your chosen location on the internet, on a streaming service, or at your local library. Talk about what you would need to pack, what sights you'd like to see, and what things you'd like to do on the ship. You may even want to look at a cruise line's website to see what cruise ships offer their passengers.

SAIL AWAY APPLE SNACKS

Make Sail Away apple snacks by combining ¼ C peanut butter, 3 Tbsp. chopped peanuts, ¼ C crispy rice cereal, and 3 Tbsp. of raisins. Cut an apple in half and scoop out the core, leaving room for the peanut butter mixture. Spoon the mixture into the apple halves. Make sails by cutting a slice of cheese into triangles. Thread it onto a toothpick, and secure one end of the toothpick into the apple. Voila! Both you and your granddaughter each have a sail away snack that includes three of the four food groups. Bon Voyage!

HOUSE OF CARDS

Take an inexpensive deck of playing cards. It's okay if it's incomplete. (You can also use a stack of 3 x 5 cards, that your granddaughter can decorate to suit her own taste.) Make a ¼" cut on the sides of each card. Then, build a tower, stacking cards by inserting them into the slits of another card. You can compete to see who can build the highest tower, but it's even more fun to work together. How high can you go? What wild designs can you make?

SHOEBOX SWEET SHOEBOX

Help your granddaughter make her own dollhouse by fashioning it out of shoeboxes. Cover the box with construction paper or color it with markers or child-safe craft paint. Allow it to dry. Lay the box on its side. Make furniture from small pieces of cardboard, plastic bottle caps, toilet paper rolls...whatever odds and ends you can find around the house. Use your imagination. Brainstorm together how you can use what you would normally throw in the trash.

Cut pictures out of magazines to make art to glue on the walls, a tablecloth for your dining table, or a bedspread to glue onto your cardboard bedroom set. Use sheets of gift wrap as wall paper. Use your miniature dolls or be creative and make your own people.

Turn your shoebox home into an apartment complex, by stacking more boxes on top, or add on other rooms with boxes of different sizes.

PAINTING WITH SAND

If you live near a beach, or are visiting one with your granddaughter, bring a plastic bag filled with sand home with you to create your own beautiful beach memory. (If the beach is too far away, you can also purchase a bag of sand at a hobby store.) Divide the sand into several smaller plastic bags. Add a few drops of food coloring to each bag. Carefully seal each bag and then shake until the color is spread throughout. Spread the sand on newspaper and allow it to dry for a few minutes. While the sand is drying, have your granddaughter use a pencil to draw a simple picture on a piece of cardboard or posterboard. Maybe she'd like to recreate the fun you two had together at the shore! When the sand is dry, put the sand back in individual plastic bags. Spread a thin layer of glue over one section of the drawing at a time. Then, sprinkle one color of sand over that section. Shake the excess sand back onto the newspaper and then put it back into its plastic bag. Have your granddaughter repeat the process until her masterpiece is complete. Allow the finished work of art about an hour to dry before putting it on display.

CELEBRATE THE 70'S

Invite your granddaughter to join you on a trip back in time! Be sure and share your own memories of that time as you help her create her own lava light. Fill an empty water bottle about 2/3 full of vegetable oil. Fill the rest with water, leaving about an inch unfilled at the top. Add your chosen color of food coloring and stir gently with a chopstick. (The food color will only mix with the water.) Break an effervescent antacid tablet into four pieces. Add one quarter at a time and watch your lava lamp begin to dance! You can reseal the bottle and save it to use again in the future. Just add another antacid tablet to get it moving!

YEAR-ROUND CELEBRATION TREE

Decorating the Christmas tree is a tradition that's always fun to share with family, including grandmothers and granddaughters. But Christmas only comes around once a year. Why not enjoy this tradition, and make new memories, year-round?

Purchase a small, tabletop tree after Christmas, when the sales are good. Then use it as your Granddaughter tree. Together, decide how you'd like to decorate it throughout the year. Here are a few ideas to get you started:

- Purchase some origami paper (or cut squares out of gift wrap or from the pages of a book you no longer use). Using a book from the library, or following lessons online, learn how to make different origami animals and shapes together. Use them to decorate your tree.

- When Autumn arrives, go on a walk and collect colorful fall leaves. Using a needle and thread, carefully make a small thread loop at the top of each leaf and tie it to your tree.

- Save paper fortunes you receive from fortune cookies and hang them from the tree!

- Create a Family Tree, by cutting out faces of your family from old photos and hanging them from the branches.

- Work together to cut out words and pictures from old magazines that represent your hopes for the coming year. Paste them on 3 x 5 cards, then trim the cards to fit the shape of the pictures. Poke a paper clip through the top of the card and use as a hanger for your Dream Tree.

TWIRLY-WHIRLY CELEBRATION TREE

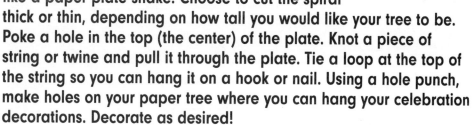

You can make a less permanent, and less expensive, alternative to the Celebration Tree by fashioning one from a paper plate. Paint or color a paper plate green. Make a spiral cut from the edge to the center of the plate, so that it dangles like a paper plate snake. Choose to cut the spiral thick or thin, depending on how tall you would like your tree to be. Poke a hole in the top (the center) of the plate. Knot a piece of string or twine and pull it through the plate. Tie a loop at the top of the string so you can hang it on a hook or nail. Using a hole punch, make holes on your paper tree where you can hang your celebration decorations. Decorate as desired!

FAMILY TREE FUN

The most important tree you and your granddaughter can create together is a representation of your family tree. Find a template on the internet or draw your own tree together on poster board, figuring out how many branches you need to include as many family members as you can. Place photos or drawings of each family member on the tree. Share stories about each family member as you go, making sure you invite your granddaughter to share her recollections, instead of simply reminiscing about your own. Your granddaughter may also want to create a small "Feels Like Family Tree." Encourage her to include images of people who feel like family, those who she looks up to, like teachers, neighbors, coaches, or mentors, as well as her circle of friends.

HAPPY HOLIDAYS WREATH

Make a quick and easy wreath by using scraps of Christmas fabric. Cut three strips of fabric 2 to 3 feet long, and at least 8 inches wide. Fold the fabric in half, lengthwise, and sew a seam down the edge of each strip. Turn them right-side out. Stuff them with batting. Braid the three strips. Bring the loose ends together to form a circle. Hand sew, or use a sewing machine, to secure all of the ends together to form a wreath. Sew a large fabric bow or a piece of artificial Christmas greenery over the part of the wreath where the edges are joined. Sew a small hook on the back of the wreath for hanging.

LONELY SOCK SNOWMAN

Use lone socks who have lost their mates somewhere along the way to make a sock snowman. Fill a clean sock, preferably white, with rice. Make it as tall, or short, as you like, secure the opening with a rubber band. (The portion of sock above the rubber band will be covered by the snowman's hat.) Then, place a rubber band around the center, making the bottom "snowball" larger than the top. Wrap a piece of ribbon around the middle rubber band. Make a face and buttons on your snowman with a permanent marker or glue on small felt cut-outs of circles, and an orange triangle for the nose. Then, cut off the toe of a colored sock, roll up the edges, and use it as a hat for your snowman. Your snowman makes a great doorstop or table decoration.

MAKING THE MOST OF CHRISTMAS MEMORIES

Making Christmas decorations with your granddaughter allows her to bring home something festive that will also remind her of you, and your times together, every time she sees it. This is a way of strengthening your relationship, even when you're apart. Here are a few quick and easy holiday projects you can enjoy creating together.

PINECONE CHRISTMAS TREES

Head out to the woods to pick up a few pinecones, while enjoying walking and talking together. When you get home, dust off any excess dirt inside the pinecones. Then, paint them green with child-safe paint, using a small paintbrush. Allow it time to dry. Next, paint the tips of the pinecone white to look like snow. Allow it time to dry. Then, with a small, round brush, paint tiny dots of bright-colored paint on the cone to look like Christmas lights. Make a stand for your pinecone tree by using a circle of thick cardboard, a coaster you no longer use, or a clear plastic, disposable dessert plate. Have Grandma use a hot glue gun to attach the bottom of your pinecone upright onto your base, holding it for a few minutes until it is sturdy enough to stand on its own.

SPARKLING SNOWFLAKES

Make snowflakes using craft sticks or clean popsicle sticks. Paint them or color them with markers. Bedazzle them with glitter, sequins, rhinestones, stickers…whatever you and your granddaughter's hearts' desire. Then, make a stack of three sticks, forming a six-point star, gluing one on top of the other. Glue a twine or Christmas ribbon loop to the top to hang it on the tree or in a window.

iCiCLE TWiSTS

Replace messy tinsel on the tree by making these simple icicle twists! Tear a triangular shape out of a piece of foil, about an inch longer than you would like your icicle to be. Shiny side down, fold the flat end about ¾ inch down, which will be the top of your icicle. This will help strengthen the area where your icicle hangs. Tape a loop of yarn, twine, or ribbon to the middle of the folded top of your triangle. Roll the folded edge of your triangle, forming a long "snake." Then, gently squeeze the foil together, squeezing the foil more loosely at the top and tightly together at the bottom to form an icicle shape. With a small paint-brush, randomly paint a thin layer on your icicle. Shake blue glitter over your icicle. Put a paper plate beneath it to contain the excess glitter. After the glue has dried, give it a good shake over the plate to remove any extra glitter.

SANTA'S BEARD COUNTDOWN

Once December begins, Christmas seems as though it's only one deep breath away. But for kids, the days seem to drag on as slow as molasses until the 25th. To help your granddaughter count down the days until the Big One arrives, make a Santa countdown calendar that she can hang in her room at home, removing one paper chain link from Santa's beard each day. Simply make a Santa face on a paper plate. Get as creative as time and interest allows, adding a construction paper hat, cotton ball hair, draw on eyes... whatever tickles your granddaughter's fancy. Then, make several paper chains of various lengths with links of white paper—24 links in all. Staple each length of chain next to each other on Santa's chin to form a "countdown" beard.

MARBLED MESSAGES

This year, take Valentines or Christmas cards to a whole new homemade level by creating marbled cardstock. You and your granddaughter will enjoy the unexpected, professional looking designs you can create with just shaving cream foam, child-safe paint, and white card stock. Spray a layer of shaving cream foam (only the FOAM will work) into a shallow baking dish or pie pan. Put a few drops of liquid watercolor paint on top of the foam and gently swirl it in with a disposable chopstick, toothpick, or the wooden end of a paintbrush. Stir gently, because you don't want to mix in the color, but leave rainbow-colored swirls.

Press the card stock onto the top of the swirled foam, let it sit for a few seconds, and then lift it back up. Scrape the excess foam off into a separate bowl. Set your marbled cardstock aside to dry. Add a few more drops of color to the foam, and swirl, after every 2 or 3 sheets. When you've finished, scrape all of the excess colored foam into the trash before washing your pans. Simply fold the cardstock in half to make a card, or cut the cardstock into shapes, like a heart or star to make flat greeting cards. You can also use a shaped hole punch on one sheet of cardstock and then glue the shapes (such as hearts, stars, angels, or Christmas tree shapes) onto your cardstock for a 3-dimensional design.

DARE TO DREAM

We are never too old, or too young, to dream! Sharing our dreams with others is not only an act of vulnerability and trust, it helps others gain a more accurate picture of who we really are. That's why making a vision board with your granddaughter is more than just a fun way to spend time together. It's an opportunity to gain a better understanding of each other's deep-seated, individual passions—without having to speak a word. However, talking about your vision boards as you're working on them is bound to happen!

Start with a plain poster board for each person. Set a stack of old magazines, scissors, colored pencils or markers, and glue sticks on the kitchen table. Then, spend some time going through the magazines, page by page, clipping words or images that spark your imagination, reflect your interests, or help illustrate what your hopes and dreams for your future happen to be. Feel free to expand your vision board by adding photos, artwork, or printouts from the internet. Anything that strikes your fancy!

As you discuss the items you both choose to include in your vision board collage, talk about what it would take to make these dreams become reality. Discuss the importance of perseverance, hard work, flexibility, optimism, and asking for help when you need it. Discuss what is realistic, and what is less likely to happen, but be careful not to squelch Big Dreams. They can come true!

Hang your Vision Boards somewhere you can see them every day. You may want to make this an annual activity. See how much your dreams change—or stay the same—year after year.

CELEBRATE THE SMALL THINGS

Why wait for a holiday to enjoy a celebration? Celebrate the little things, like your granddaughter getting a perfect score on her spelling test, learning how to master the yoyo, or even having a "Great Attitude" day. Go ahead, bring out the berries and bubbly. Add a maraschino cherry and a Tbsp. of cherry juice to lemon-lime soda and serve it in a fancy flute. Make chocolate covered strawberries or pitted cherries by putting melted chocolate in an ice cube tray. Then put a strawberry or cherry into each compartment, submerging half of it in the chocolate and leaving the stem side sticking out. Chill in the fridge just until the chocolate hardens, about 15 to 30 minutes. Pop out of the tray and eat right away, or store in an airtight container in a cool place. (The fridge is too cold and will make the chocolate taste chalky.)

TINFOIL TROPHY

Go one step further in celebrating your granddaughter by presenting her with a trophy fashioned out of tinfoil. Then, have her think of trophy-worthy kindnesses or accomplishments that the other members of her family deserve. Help her fashion her own tinfoil trophies, listing the recipient and reason for this special recognition on 3 x 5 cards. Tear off squares of foil in a manageable size to work with. For even more of a challenge, have her try making a tinfoil tiara!

Games & Things to pass the Time

If you and your granddaughter find yourself just hanging out together while waiting for an appointment or standing in line, here are a few ideas on how you can turn those "wasted" moments into more memorable ones, plus more fun projects to do together at home.

MAGIC FINGERS

Ask your granddaughter to put her fists together, with the fingers touching. Then point both of the index fingers up toward the sky. Stand in front of her and twirl your index finger quickly around her index fingers. Watch her fingers automatically move closer together. Then trade places!

THANKFUL

Take turns naming something you're thankful for. It can be as small as being thankful that you're wearing comfortable shoes or as big as being grateful for the gift of being related to one another. Anyone who ends up stumped, loses. But chances are, your time will run out before your reasons for being thankful do.

RHYME TIME

Take turns making up two-word rhymes, such as "cake snake" or "snore chore." They don't have to make sense. The crazier the better. To make the game more difficult, start with one syllable words, then proceed to two, and then three. For instance, "swell smell," then "poodle noodle," and "cockatoo flockaroo." Be creative and draw what your "rhyme character" would look like.

RHYMING i SPY

Here's a twist on an old favorite. Choose something you both can see, then give each other clues to help the other person guess your chosen item. For instance, if you're at the bank waiting in line, you could say, "I rhyme with honey" to help your granddaughter guess, "money." Or, "I rhyme with a mean squirt" for a green shirt.

LAZY DAISY

Another variation on a rhyming word game is played by giving clues that describe a pair of rhyming words, such as "a couch potato flower." That would be a lazy daisy. Or how about a "record player who refused to change out of her nightgown"? That's a PJ DJ. "A hamster caught in a rainstorm"? A "wet pet."

A SHOW OF HANDS

Bring out the washable paints! Then, using a large piece of paper or cardboard, work together with your granddaughter to make a picture using both of your handprints. What will it be? Right-side up it's a turkey. Turn it on its side and make a bird, with the thumb for a beak and feathers fashioned from the fingers sticking out the back. How about funny faces with wild "finger" hair? Finish off the picture using just your fingerprints to make flowers, butterflies or people.

You can also use your handprints as "frames" for messages to each other. Cut a heart shape out of cardstock, and write a special message to each other on it. For example, "Hands down, you're the greatest granddaughter around!" or "When I'm too far away to hold your hand, I'll always hold you in my heart." Then glue the message on the palm of your handprint.

POETRY CORNER

Do you have a favorite poem? Share it with your granddaughter, including why it's so special to you. Then, talk about different forms of poetry, such as haiku, limericks, sonnets, cinquain, etc. Using a book of poetry, or poems found on the internet, have your granddaughter find some she enjoys. Then, help her create a poetry book of her own. Have your granddaughter organize her favorite poems into the pages of a blank book, challenging her to write a few originals of her own—discussing what inspired her to choose these topics and forms.

PAPER PLATE FLYER

When the weather is nice, it's good for the soul to head outside and enjoy a little outdoor activity together with your granddaughter. Here's something that's active, but not overly so. First, you'll need a little indoor time together assembling your paper plate flyers. Color the bottom of two paper plates with crayons or markers. Cut a large circle out of the center of the plate—about ⅔ the size of the plate. Invert the plates, and then Grandma hot glue's them together, bottom sides facing out. Allow the glue to dry. Take your paper plate flyer outside and sail it to each other just like a store-bought plastic disc.

ALIEN PIE IN THE SKY

Here's a variation on the paper plate flyer that looks like an alien craft. Color both sides of a paper plate. Then, draw a circle on the center of the plate that covers about ⅔ of the plate's size. Draw lines that divide the circle into 12 equal triangles, like pieces of pie. Cut each "slice" from the center towards the edge of the circle, keeping the pieces attached to the flyer at the outer edge. Then, alternate folding one triangle up and the next down. While you and your granddaughter try sailing it to each other, talk about the world beyond this one. Do you believe there is life on other planets? Why or why not? Would you journey into space if you had the opportunity?

FUN WAYS & FUN DAYS WITH CLAY

Many child-safe brands and kinds of clay are available in craft and hobby stores. Polymer clay, a popular choice, works for various projects. After kneading a lump, it softens and becomes a versatile sculpting medium. Even if you take your time molding, polymer clay will remain malleable. It will harden as it bakes in the oven. (Grandma should supervise when using the oven.)

Air-dry clay is also easy and fun to work with. Unlike a polymer clay, however, it hardens as it dries, so there is no need for baking.

You can find both clays in a range of colors.

Or, you and your granddaughter can mix up your own clay with ingredients right in your kitchen!

There are several ways to make clay using only flour or cornstarch, baking soda, and water. Food coloring is optional. Two recipes are printed here, but many more can be found online.

Recipe 1
1 cup cornstarch
2 cups baking soda
1 1/2 cups cold water
Food coloring (optional)

Mix all ingredients together in a saucepan over low heat, stir until a dough forms. Remove from heat and cover with a damp towel, allowing it to cool before use.

Recipe 2
4 cups flour
1 cup salt
1 1/2 cups water
Food coloring (optional)

Mix all ingredients together in a bowl to make the clay. Sculpt, then bake sculpted pieces on a non-stick cookie sheet for about an hour at 350°. Place on a wire rack to cool.

Clay pieces can be decorated using acrylics, tempera paints, poster paint, or nail polish. (Note: acrylic paints are not washable, so cover clothing and work surfaces when working with it.) Store leftover clay in a tightly sealed container or follow directions carefully if using purchased clay so it stays moist and usable.

GG PLAQUE

Celebrate your relationship in an artistic way to come up with a GG (Grandmother/Granddaughter) motto that is unique to you. It could be as simple as "Old + Young = FUN!" or "3,245 miles apart, but always close at heart!" Once you've come up with your motto, why not make a clay plaque so you can put it on display?

You'll need clay, texturing tools (such as a fork, butter knife, spoon, paper clip, a wooden dowel, pencil, toothpicks, etc.), a pencil or straw to make a hole for hanging, and string, yarn, or a strand of leather to hang your plaque from. Roll out two rectangles of clay, one larger than the other, about ¼" thick. Texturize the edges of the larger rectangle to make a "frame." Write your motto in the smaller rectangle, using a wooden dowel, pencil, or butter knife. If you like, add the date and decorative symbols or designs.

Then, place the smaller rectangle on the larger "frame" and gently press the two rectangles together. Use a straw or the eraser end of a pencil to make a hole in the top center of the plaque for hanging. When the plaque is hardened and completely dry, paint it as desired.

Giggles 'n' Grins

What is an owl's favorite
kind of a movie?
A whooo-dunnit.

Why did the horse
cross the road?
To reach his neigh-borhood.

What do the moon and a
dollar have in common?
They both have four
quarters.

When does money fall
from the sky?
When there's a change
in the weather.

What kind of tree can you
hold in your hand?
A palm tree.

What kind of flowers are
on your face?
Tulips.

What's the Milky Way's favorite key on
the computer keyboard?
The space bar.

What season is it
when you play on a
trampoline?
Springtime.

What goes around
a yard but never
moves?
A fence.

How did the tree get on the internet?
It logged in.

What is the hardest
thing about learning
to ride a bike?
The pavement.

If a farmer raises wheat
in dry weather, what does
he raise in wet weather?
His umbrella.

What did the Sun
say when it was
introduced to
the Earth?
Nice to heat you!

What falls but
never hits the
ground?
The temperature.

HOW DOES GRANDMA'S GARDEN GROW?

If gardening is something you enjoy, involve your granddaughter in planning what you will plant in the season ahead. Will it be a wildflower garden? A vegetable garden? A butterfly garden? Where will you plant each item? Talk about how much water, and sun or shade, each of these plants needs. Decide whether you want to grow your garden from seeds or from plants that have already sprouted. Then, work on planting your garden together. If your granddaughter doesn't live nearby, send her photos of how Grandma's garden is growing. If what you plant is edible, be sure to include it on the menu when your granddaughter comes to visit.

SPRINGTIME, ANYTIME

Most grandmothers don't have the privilege of seeing their granddaughter every day, or even every week. Why not plant flower bulbs to help count down the passage of time until your next visit? Tulips and daffodils are hardy choices and bloom in about 4 to 6 weeks. About a month before your granddaughter's visit, put the bulbs in a bowl of pebbles and water. Be sure that the base of the bulb is wet at all times. Put the bowl in a dark place for about 10 days, until the roots form. Then, move them to a sunny windowsill and watch for the first glimpse of green to appear. Send your granddaughter a weekly photo of the bulb's growth, counting down the days until you get to see each other again.

A SOCK WALK GARDEN

Invite your granddaughter to join you for a walk—in her socks! Before you head out, prepare a moist soil-mix box where your sock garden can grow. Then, head out to a neighborhood park or a wooded path. When you get there, put a large pair of old cotton socks over your granddaughter's shoes, and yours. Then, enjoy your walk together!

Talk about what your socks are picking up from the path…seeds, grasses, soil, leaves, etc. When you get back home, plant your socks in the soil and watch what grows! Keep the box moist and warm. Indoors is best. Note: If you're wearing thin cotton socks, you can plant the whole sock in the box and cover it with about an inch of soil. If you're wearing thick cotton socks, like tube socks, cut off just the sole to plant.

NATURE BRACELET

Add a homemade bracelet to your outdoor adventure by securing a piece of packing tape or masking tape (sticky side out) around your granddaughter's wrist before heading out. (You may want to cut it in half if the width is uncomfortable on your granddaughter's wrist.) Then, along your walk, have your granddaughter "pick up" little bits of nature by touching them with her sticky wristband, until her entire bracelet is covered.

NATURAL MOBILE

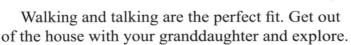

Walking and talking are the perfect fit. Get out of the house with your granddaughter and explore. Talk about what you see…the different shapes, colors, how things are changing with the seasons. Pick up some little treasures along the way, such as stones, seed pods, leaves, twigs—or seashells if you happen to live by the shore. Then work together to make a mobile of your finds. Using wire, string, or twine, hang them on a rod or stick, or hang them from the branches of a tree in your yard, as a memento of your time together.

KISSED BY THE BREEZE

If the weather is mild and there's a gentle breeze blowing, take a close-up look at nature in your own backyard. Put a white sheet down on the ground and lie down on it with your granddaughter. Watch the clouds sail by, sharing what creatures—real or mythical—you see in their shapes. Share a picnic lunch, if you like. After a while, see what has blown onto your sheet. Insects? Leaves? Pollen? Look closely at them with a magnifying glass. Draw pictures of what you discovered once you head back inside.

I SPY A BIRD IN THE SKY

Bird watching is a pastime as old as the hills. Introduce your granddaughter to the wide variety of species liable to frequent your area by checking out a book from the library, looking on the internet, or picking up a pamphlet on local wildlife from a park service near you. Then, spend some time walking the neighborhood, hanging out in your yard, or simply looking through a picture window into a garden area. See how many you can spy together. Which species do you see most frequently? Which ones migrate? Which is your favorite and why?

FEED THE BIRDS

Once you and your granddaughter are familiar with the birds in your area, go a step further and invite them to dinner! Spread a layer of peanut butter over an empty toilet paper roll, then roll it in birdseed. Slip the "snack" over the branch of a tree and wait for your newly found feathered friends to arrive!

FEED THE BiRDS A BiT MORE

You and your granddaughter will enjoy making these fancifully-shaped bird snacks. In a large bowl, dissolve 2 packets of gelatin in a few Tbsps. of boiling water. Stir gently until the gelatin is totally dissolved. Add 2 cups of birdseed. Stir until the gelatin and seed are thoroughly mixed. Lay out cookie cutters or pancake molds on a parchment paper-covered tray. Using a teaspoon, fill the molds so they are overflowing a bit. Then, using another sheet of parchment paper, press down the seed mixture, making sure it is tightly packed into the mold. (The more tightly they are packed, the better they will stay together when they are hanging.) Cut a straw into 4-inch pieces. Press the straw through the mixture near the top of the mold, not too close to the edge. Press the mixture down again. Put the tray with the molds in the fridge for a couple of hours. Then, let the birdseed snacks dry on the counter overnight. The next morning, gently pop the treats out of the mold and take out the straws. Tie ribbon, string, or twine through the hole and hang your treats outside in a tree or from the eaves of your home, on a hook, rod, or twine hooked onto a nail.

SODA BOTTLE FEEDER

You and your granddaughter can make a refillable feeder using a plastic soda bottle and 2 old wooden spoons. Cut a small circular hole about 4 inches from the bottom of a 20 oz. plastic soda bottle. Make sure it is large enough to fit the handle of your wooden spoon. On the opposite side, cut another hole, slightly larger, where the birdseed will spill out into the bowl of your spoon. Cut another set of holes about 2 inches below these holes, on the opposite side of the bottle, about 90 degrees from the first holes. Place your two wooden spoons through the holes. Fill the bottle with birdseed. Secure floral wire, twine, or string to the top of the bottle, leaving a length long enough to secure to the branch of a tree. Put the lid back on the bottle and your bird buffet is ready to hang!

BiRD CoLLAGE

After spending time watching birds together, why not create a few of your own? Use cupcake papers to create them. Fold the papers in half to fashion whimsical wings and bodies. Use a variety of colors and patterns, gluing them onto construction paper, poster board, or pieces of cardboard. Draw in your finishing touches to complete your picture. Create images of the birds you've seen together or a fantastical bird given birth by your own imagination?

NATURE AS ART

If your granddaughter is going to spend a few days with you, here is a project you can work on throughout your visit. Go on walks together, gathering small found objects to bring home, such as leaves, seed pods, pebbles, and wildflowers. Place the flowers and leaves between two sheets of wax paper, and place them inside, or under, a heavy book or other weighty item. Allow them to dry, and flatten, for a few days.

Then, use a piece of foam board or poster board as the surface where you'll secure your found items for your nature collage. (If you'd like to display your collage, and protect your 3-D items, find a shadow box frame that fits the size of your collage board.) Glue them in place. To help secure heavier objects, such as pebbles, Grandma can use a hot glue gun.

Make an abstract collage or use the found objects to make a scene. For instance, stack small stones to make people and glue a leaf above them. Draw a line from the leaf to a stone person, to make the leaf resemble a kite. Add a tail beneath the leaf kite by either drawing it in or using small pieces of twig. Or make a scene representing your granddaughter and yourself.

A GIVING GARDEN

Everyone enjoys the gift of a flower! Instead of spending money on a bouquet from the store or plucking them from your own garden, why not spend a bit of time creating Grandmother/Granddaughter originals from paper plates? Brainstorm with your granddaughter individuals who you think would enjoy this homemade gift of Spring. A neighbor? Residents at a rest home? Members of your own family? Deliver them together, accompanied by the gift of a warm smile.

Cut the edges of four paper plates into petal shapes, with the petals on each plate cut a bit smaller than the last.

Glue the center of the plates together, the largest petaled plate on the bottom and the smallest on the top.

Once the glue has dried, curl the edges of the flower petals with your finger or by rolling it around a pencil. Then, use your imagination to decorate! Color in the center using a marker, or glue small dots of construction paper made from a hole punch, a colorful circle of fabric, a bottle cap...what else can you think of? Leave the rest of the flower white or paint or color as desired.

If you'd like to make your flowers even more distinctive, glue pictures or designs from magazine pages onto the paper plate before cutting the petals. Try different color combinations or themes, such as different shades of blue or different pictures all having to do with the beach.

FASHION BASKET

Before you donate old clothing, jewelry, or accessories to a local charity, give them one more go-around by adding them to a dress-up basket or box for your granddaughter. You may also want to add a few fun and funky finds from your local thrift shop to the mix. Bring out the Fashion Basket any time your granddaughter is ready for a little dress-up fun. Give her different challenges, like these:

• Dress—and then act—like someone you're both familiar with, whether a member of the family, a celebrity, or a historical figure. Can the other person guess who you are?

• Use the Fashion Basket to see who can create the wackiest, scariest, or most fashionable outfit.

• Each of you put on an outfit with the same number of pieces—then see who can take the outfit off and put it back on inside-out in the fastest time.

• Become a new person! Dress up and give yourself a new name and personality. Then sit down for snacks or a cup of tea and carry on a conversation, staying in character.

EASY OUTSIDE ADVENTURES

If you and your granddaughter need to get out of the house and get your blood pumping, here are a few easy adventures you can experience right outside your front door.

• Have a windy day dance contest. Grab scarves, crepe paper, or even plastic grocery bags. Then turn on the music and get moving! A few minutes of dancing will lighten your mood and add some extra smiles to your day. If you care to share those smiles, make a video of your granddaughter dancing to share with her parents or friends.

• Grab the sidewalk chalk and create a work of art. Write a positive message on your driveway for passersby to enjoy. Take the time to create a scene together, each of you drawing a separate part of the picture. Get into the picture by drawing a bunch of balloons, a dog on a leash, or a rocket ship heading for space. Then lie down on the ground, so it looks like you're part of the picture and take some interactive photos.

• Draw a chalk hopscotch grid and show your granddaughter how to play something you enjoyed as a child.

• Blowing bubbles isn't just for little kids. Bring out a bottle of bubbles and take turns blowing them, seeing how far they go, how big they get, and how many you can create from one blow. If you don't have any bubble solution on hand, make your own. Combine 6 C of water, 1 C of dish soap, and ¼ C of corn syrup.

Stir gently—then blow! Blowing bubbles is not only relaxing, it also provides a beautiful backdrop for an easygoing, conversation between the two of you.

• Make your own personalized walking sticks. Head out for a walk at a park or open space where sticks abound. Search for a stick that fits your height. On the way home, talk about how you're going to "make it your own." If you want to paint it or embellish it with permanent markers, help your granddaughter remove any bark with a paint scraper, or piece of sandpaper. Attach crepe paper streamers tacked near the top of the stick. Using clear packing tape or strong, all-purpose glue, attach shells, feathers, photos, stickers, or rhinestones. Try and out-bling one another!

• If the weather is warm, grab some kitchen sponges and make your own Spongey Spiders. Cut colorful dish sponges into four pieces lengthwise. Stack two layers of four pieces of sponge on top of each other. Tie them around the middle with a piece of strong string or fishing line. Head outdoors with a bucket of water. Soak your Spongey Spiders, then toss them back and forth, or use them to play a silly, soggy game of dodgeball. Expect to get wet—and have a great time doing it!

• Make sock puppets out of old, clean socks you no longer use. Create different characters. Try making one to represent each member of your family! Make facial features by drawing them on with permanent markers. Attach yarn hair or anything else that will give your characters personality. Then, ad lib a play on the front porch. Or head to the park, sit behind a bench, and pop up your puppets when people walk by to give an impromptu show. It's a sure way to share a smile with each other, as well as anyone who happens to walk by.

GRAND GALLERY

If your granddaughter enjoys art, help expand her creative horizons by encouraging her to venture outside the paint box! Here are a few ideas to help get you started. Just remember this isn't a spectator sport. Doing an art project with your granddaughter, instead of simply giving her directions on how to complete it by herself, helps nurture a deeper relationship. Be open with your failures, as well as your successes. Your example will help her feel freer to be more open and vulnerable with you.

BEAUTIFUL BRUSH UPS

Put aside the traditional paintbrush for a while and try something a bit unconventional, instead. Use a small bundle of uncooked spaghetti for a brush. Dip interlocking plastic blocks, nail heads, bent paperclips, or disposable plastic silverware to paint or "stamp" a picture. Try cotton swabs, small pieces cut from a clean sponge, a handful of zip-ties, or old make-up sponges and brushes (cleaned with soap and hot water). Work together with your granddaughter to invent different kinds of unconventional brushes. Combine different types of brushwork to create a one-of-a-kind masterpiece.

ABSTRACT DRIP PAINTINGS

Head outside to create some awesome abstract art. Hang a large sheet of paper from a clothesline or on a string tied between two patio chairs. Fill several squeeze bottles or old, clean shampoo bottles, with paint. Put an old sheet or newspaper beneath the hanging paper. Then, have fun squeezing paint on the paper and allowing it to drip down the page. Layer colors, allowing each layer time to dry before applying the next color. Then, rehang the paper on its side, and continue the process until your work of art is complete.

CRAZY KEYS

If your granddaughter is old enough to have her own house keys, why not help her set them apart with a bright bit of bling? Paint the top of the key (not the notched edge) with nail polish. If you are choosing to use more than one color, wait until the first color dries. Then go wild. Add polka dots, animal stripes, or smiley faces. You can even glue on a rhinestone or two, if she's a sparkly girl.

A variation on this idea is for you and your granddaughter to swap the key to each other's heart. Find two old keys you no longer use. Decorate a key for your granddaughter and have her decorate one for you. Feel free to bling it out from top to bottom! String a colorful piece of yarn through the top. Wear it as a necklace or hang it from a hook in your room. Either way, it's a beautiful reminder of how much love each of you have unlocked in each other.

SIMPLE SUNCATCHERS

Here's something you can hang in your window as a reminder of your granddaughter's visit or she can bring home to decorate her room. You'll need a large bottle of white glue, food color, toothpicks, and a disposable plastic lid. Pour a generous amount of glue into the plastic lid, filling the bottom completely. Add 1 to 2 drops of food color and swirl them into the glue with a toothpick. Encourage your granddaughter to use restraint, so that she doesn't dye all of the glue one color, but simply leaves swirls of color. Swirl in other colors, if desired. Allow to dry completely. The suncatcher is dry when it easily pulls away from the plastic lid. Either stick a paper clip through it to make a loop you can tie a string through or use a hole punch to make a hole to thread string through.

YARN ART

If your granddaughter has an artist's heart, and you're looking for new ways to help her express herself (with minimal mess), try painting with yarn. All you need is a clear, self-adhesive book cover (the sticky side of a self-adhesive shelf liner will also work) and brightly colored pieces of yarn cut into a variety of different lengths.
Using small pieces of tape, secure the corners of the book cover (sticky-side up) to a larger sheet of paper or cardboard. This will make it easier for your granddaughter to move the painting around as she's putting the yarn in place.

Then it's time to experiment! Have your granddaughter "draw" a picture by sticking the yarn pieces onto the adhesive surface. First, "draw" the basic outline of the subject. Then, add another piece of yarn right next to each part of the outline, "shadowing" it. Continue filling in the spaces and shadowing the lines until the entire surface is covered. Or try something less literal. Make an abstract scene, winding the yarn into different shapes in any way that strikes your granddaughter's fancy. If your budding artist changes her mind along the way, don't worry. The yarn can easily be removed and replaced, to make something new.

PLEIN AIR ADVENTURE

Take your artwork outside, just like Monet, Pissarro, and Renoir did in days gone by. Armed with a sketchbook and a pencil, take a walk with your granddaughter, searching for the "perfect spot" where you can sit and draw what you see around you. Bring along a blanket to toss on the ground—and maybe some snacks. (Let's face it, snacks make everything more fun!) Then, just draw. You can choose to try and capture the entire scene or simply sketch little details of flowers, leaves, rocks…whatever inspires you. Don't worry about doing it "right." Simply have fun! On the way home, talk about what you enjoyed the most, what part of Plein Air was the hardest, and what you created that you're most proud of.

EASY BATIK TEE

Although traditional batik involves hot wax and dye, here is an easy alternative that takes a lot less time and makes a lot less mess. It will take several days to complete, however, so make certain your granddaughter's visit is long enough for her to finish her new shirt! You'll need a white tee shirt, child-safe fabric paints, cardboard, tacks, a grocery bag, and washable blue gel glue. (Regular white glue will not work.) Stretch out your white tee on a piece of cardboard, and Grandma using tape to hold the corners in place and make a taut drawing surface. Put a brown grocery bag inside the tee to keep the front and back from adhering to each other.

Draw lines with the glue. Get creative! Draw a picture. Write a meaningful saying or commemorate a special event. Outline a self-portrait. Go full-abstract and make glue squiggles any which way. Allow to dry overnight. Then, paint the shirt with child-safe fabric paint. You can stay inside the paint lines or over the top of them. Either works! Allow to dry completely. Then soak overnight in a bucket of warm water. Pull off any bits of glue that have not dissolved in the water overnight, revealing the distinctive white "batik" lines. Wash and wear proudly for years to come!

PAPER MACHE PLAY

Paper mache (the English adaptation of the French term papi-er-mâché) is a versatile crafting technique that you and your grand-daughter can enjoy experimenting with together. You can make gifts for friends and family, masks, decorative bowls to spruce up your home décor, or lightweight sculptures of anything your mind can imagine. Choose your preferred paste, base layer form, and paper—then it's time to play! Here are a few basics to help you get started.

PAPER MACHE PASTE: You can purchase pre-made glue mix at a hobby or craft store, or easily create your own. The easiest meth-od combines 2 parts flour with 3 parts water. Stir until it achieves a glue-like texture. If it's too thin, add more flour. Too thick? Add more water. For a sturdier, more traditional paste, combine ½ C flour with 2 C of cold water. Boil 2 C of water and then add the flour/cold water mixture. Bring it back to a boil. Remove from the heat and add 3 Tbsp. of sugar. Let it cool. If you live in a humid climate, add a dash of salt to prevent the paste from molding. Keep any leftover paste in the refrigerator until your next Grandmother and Grand-daughter project.

PAPER: Traditionally, strips of newspaper (about 1" wide, of differing lengths) are the preferred medium, but they're not the only paper able to create a beautiful work of art. Try tissue paper, gift wrap, lightweight card stock, pages from catalogs or magazines, and even the pulp from cardboard egg cartons. If you want to paint your finished creation, put a layer of white paper towel strips over your newspaper layer, so the newsprint won't show through. But consider allowing the paper you choose to become an integral part of your design, whether it's the headlines from the morning news or a patch-work of patterns from photos featured in a magazine spread.

BASE LAYER FORM: This is the structure you will wrap your paper strips around to give it the shape you want. You can fashion a structure from wire, using a thin wire coat hanger. Another traditional form favorite is an inflated balloon, which you pop before removing your dry, finished paper mache creation. Or try using any cast-off "shape" that can be easily removed, such as a shoe box, milk carton, paper towel tubes, tin can, or crumpled newspaper. You can also use the bottom of a glass bowl or vase to make beautiful bowls of your own. Simply cover the glass with a layer of aluminum foil before adding your paste-coated paper. If you'd like to add an interesting texture, crumple the foil before covering your glass base layer. Then, add your paste-coated paper strips.

A Few Tips:
• Cover your work surface with a plastic trash bag before you begin.
• When you dip your paper into your paste mixture, make sure it's well-coated, but not saturated. Remove any excess paste with your fingers before layering it over your base form.
• Although paper mache traditionally uses torn strips of paper, try using different shapes. Cut leaf shapes out of Autumn-inspired colored cardstock. Since cardstock is sturdier than newsprint, you don't have to cover the form completely. Leave a few openings over your balloon or glass-bowl shaped form to create a beautiful filigree effect. Or use a large hole punch to cut circles or shapes from brightly patterned magazine pages. Layer over each other to create a mixed-print masterpiece.
• Allow your creation to dry overnight before removing it from your frame. (If you are using a wire frame, there's no need to remove it. Make sure the frame is completely covered with paper strips and then leave it inside.)
• If you wish to paint your creation, make certain it is dry. Acrylic paint works well but is permanent so be sure to cover clothing and surfaces.
• Seal your finished work with two or three coats of varnish or gesso, allowing each coat time to dry before adding the next one.

Giggles 'n' Grins

What vegetable is the
kindest?
A sweet potato.

What kind of fish goes best
with peanut butter?
Jellyfish.

What did the nut say
when it sneezed?
Cashew!

How do you fix a
broken pizza?
With tomato paste.

How many items
can you put in an empty
grocery bag?
One, because after you
put it in, it isn't empty
anymore.

How do shellfish get to
the hospital?
They take a clambulance.

What did the grandma ghost tell the granddaughter ghost at the dinner table?
Stop goblin your food.

What's more useful after it's broken?
An egg.

What do you get if you cross a snake with dessert?
A pie-thon.

Which friends should you always invite to dinner?
Your taste buds.

Why do little lobsters refuse to share their toys?
Because they're shellfish.

Why did the mushroom get invited to the party?
Because he's a fun-guy.

How do you make an apple turnover?
Push it downhill.

 *Grandma, please use all caution when in the kitchen, and take charge of any steps requiring heat, microwave, boiling, and sharp utensils. Make any recipe substitutions needed if your granddaughter has allergies to peanut butter, gluten, etc.*

TRADE IN THAT PB & J

It's easy to fall into the rut of simply throwing together a peanut butter and jelly sandwich for lunch when your granddaughter comes to visit. With just a bit more time and thought, you can serve up something that may become a newfound favorite. Help your granddaughter think outside the lunch box with these easy, healthy alternatives.

NANA WRAPS

Combine 2 Tbsp. of nut butter (or "no nut" butter, if your granddaughter is allergic to nuts) and 1 Tbsp. of melted dark chocolate chips on a 7" flour tortilla. Place a peeled banana on the edge of the tortilla and roll it up. You can wrap this in plastic wrap and place it in the fridge until lunchtime, if you like. Cut it in half to serve. If your granddaughter likes coconut, add 2 tsp. of shredded coconut to the nut butter and chocolate mixture for a little extra crunch.

RICOTTA TOAST

Mix ½ C ricotta with 1 tsp. honey and a dash of black pepper. Spread it over two slices of toasted whole grain bread. Slice 4 strawberries, placing two sliced berries on each slice of bread. Top with a sprinkle of chopped pistachios.

KID-FRIENDLY KABOBS

Everything's more fun on a stick! Use your imagination (and whatever you happen to have in the fridge) to create a granddaughter-friendly alternative to yet another sandwich. Try cubes of cheese, leftover chicken, rolls of deli meat, cherry tomatoes, grapes, slices of cucumber, or olives. Better yet, put everything out on the table and let your granddaughter come up with her own custom creation. Have her direct you as to how you should arrange her choices onto a wooden skewer.

Instead of just serving your granddaughter something to eat, working together to create a tasty treat makes more than a meal. It also makes happy memories!

NUTTY BUDDY BRITTLE

Since this candy involves mixtures dissolved at high temperatures, Grandma, you take the lead in preparing it! Then, have fun allowing your granddaughter to break the brittle into pieces after it's cooled. To begin, simply spread 2¼ C of your favorite nuts on a large, buttered cookie sheet. Set aside. Stir 1 C of granulated sugar, 1 C of brown sugar, ½ C light corn syrup, and 1 C water over low heat until the sugar has dissolved. Heat until the mixture reaches 240° on a candy thermometer. This will take about 15 minutes. Continue cooking another 10 to 15 minutes, stirring occasionally, until the syrup begins to turn a golden color. Stir in 1 tsp. of butter and ½ tsp. of baking soda. Immediately, pour the mixture over your nuts. After the brittle hardens, break it into pieces. Store it in an airtight container.

CHOCOLATE ICE CREAM SHELLS

Making a hard chocolate shell to top your ice cream cone or sundae is quick, easy, and so much fun to eat. Microwave 1 C of semisweet chocolate chips, 2 Tbsp. of coconut oil, and a dash of salt on high for about 1 minute, until melted. Stop the microwave every 15 seconds and give your chocolate sauce a good stir. When it's done, spoon the sauce over your favorite ice cream treat. It will harden in about 30 seconds.

mAGiC mARSHMALLOW PUFFS

Here's a snack and a magic trick, all rolled into one! Open a package of roll and bake crescent-shaped dinner rolls. Divide the rolls into individual triangles. Combine ¼ cup sugar and 1 tsp. cinnamon in a small bowl. Melt ¼ cup of butter. Dip large marshmallows into melted butter and then roll in cinnamon sugar mixture. Wrap a dough triangle around the marshmallow, completely covering it, and squeeze the edges tight. Dip filled roll in melted butter and place the roll, butter side down, in a muffin tin. Place muffin pan on a cookie sheet or sheet of foil in a pre-heated oven at 375° for 10 to 15 minutes, until golden brown. If desired, make glaze by mixing ½ cup powdered sugar, 2 to 3 tsp. of milk, and ½ tsp. vanilla in a small bowl. Drizzle glaze over slightly cooled puffs. When your granddaughter bites into the sweet treat, ask her where the disappearing marshmallow went!

PBP BARS

Chocolate, peanut butter, and pretzels go together as well as you and your granddaughter! You'll both find this no-bake treat easy to make—and even easier to eat. Line a 9 x 13 pan with foil, letting the ends hang over the sides. Set aside 1½ C of mini-pretzels for the topping, and pulse the remaining mini-pretzels from a 16 oz. bag in a food processor or blender until they become fine crumbs. Transfer them to a large bowl. Mix in 1½ C melted butter, 1½ C peanut butter, and 3 C confectioner's sugar. Press mixture into the foil-lined pan. Melt 2 C semi-sweet chocolate chips and 1 Tbsp. of shortening, stirring until smooth. Spread over the peanut butter pretzel layer. Break the reserved 1½ C mini-pretzels into pieces and sprinkle them over the top. Cover with foil and refrigerate until set, about 1 hour. Lift out the foil and cut your treat into bars.

PIE CAKE

If you and your granddaughter can't decide which is better—pie or cake—here's a way you can enjoy both! Grease a 9 x 13 pan. Put 4 C of mini-marshmallows into the pan. Prepare a boxed cake mix according to the directions. Pour it over the marshmallows. Spoon a can of pie filling evenly over the top. Bake at 350° for 50 minutes or until a toothpick comes out clean. Cool. Then top with whipped topping and serve. What flavor combinations can you come up with? If you can't decide, a few sure-fire combinations are: chocolate cake with cherry pie filling, spice cake with apple pie filling, and lemon cake with blueberry pie filling.

PINEAPPLE ANGEL CAKE

Here's an easy cake that a granddaughter of almost any age can help you bake! Mix 1 box of angel food cake mix (dry) with a 20 oz. can of crushed pineapple in juice, un-drained. Mix for 30 seconds on low speed, then 1 minute on medium speed. Pour into a 9 x 13, ungreased cake pan. Bake at 325° for 30 to 35 minutes, until golden brown and not sticky to touch. Cool. Top with whipped topping and serve.

READY FOR SECONDS CHOCOLATE

Beat together 1 box chocolate cake mix, ¾ C vegetable oil, 4 eggs, 1 small box instant chocolate pudding, 1 C of water, and 8 oz. of sour cream. Stir in 6 oz. of chocolate chips. Pour into a well-greased Bundt pan. Bake at 350° for 45 to 50 minutes. When cool, sprinkle powdered sugar on top.

MAKE YOUR OWN ICE CREAM

Imagine! Your granddaugher can make her own ice cream—right in a plastic bag!

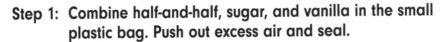

You will need:
- 1 cup half-and-half
- 2 tablespoons sugar
- 1/2 teaspoon vanilla extract
- 3 cups of ice
- 1/3 cup kosher salt
- Small plastic sandwich bag
- Large plastic storage bag

Step 1: Combine half-and-half, sugar, and vanilla in the small plastic bag. Push out excess air and seal.

Step 2: Combine ice and salt in the large plastic bag.

Step 3: Place the small bag inside the bigger bag and shake really, really hard for at least ten minutes, until the ice cream has hardened. You and your granddaughter can take turns.

Step 4: Add your favorite toppings and enjoy!

If your granddaughter is lactose intolerant, create a delicious, dairy-free, gluten-free treat, using a surprise ingredient—bananas!

Just peel a few bananas and place them in the freezer until they are frozen solid. Then place the bananas in a blender and mix well. You can eat the mixture right away if you like the soft-serve consistency. Or freeze it in an airtight container if you like your frozen treat harder. Either way, it's delicious—and healthy!

CREEPY GARDEN GOODIES

BUGS!: Spread cream cheese or peanut butter on a piece of celery. Use slices of cucumber, cherry tomatoes, berries, raisins, or grapes to fashion fantastical edible bugs. If you have decorative candy eyes on hand, secure them on a grape or tomato with peanut butter or honey to make your garden critters even more inviting.

SPIDER: Spread peanut butter on a round cracker. Place thin pretzel sticks around the edges for legs. Spread peanut butter on another cracker and use it to top the first. Attach raisins or chocolate chips with peanut butter on top for eyes. For a less sugary snack, substitute hummus for peanut butter.

CATERPILLAR: Place a line of green grapes on a wooden skewer. (Soaking the skewers for about 15 minutes in cold water will prevent splinters!) Put half of a strawberry at the end of your caterpillar. Break a pretzel stick in half and use each half as an antenna for your caterpillar. Use a toothpick to put two small dabs of cream cheese on the strawberry to attach mini chocolate chip eyes.

SAY "CHEESE!"

Grilled cheese sandwiches and macaroni and cheese are time-tested grandkid favorites. But that doesn't mean they can't use a little upgrade now and then. Here are a few ways you and your granddaughter can try a new twist on a family favorite!

GOURMET GRILLED CHEESE

• Instead of simply buttering the bread before grilling it, dip it in beaten egg and then shredded parmesan cheese. Add some deli turkey, ham, or roast beef inside with your cheese.

• Spread the inside of both slices of bread with apple butter or cranberry sauce, then layer brie, turkey, thinly sliced gala apple, and baby greens.

• Try layering brie, basil, blueberry preserves and brown sugar on buttered white bread!

• Spread the inside of both slices of bread with fig jam, then layer deli turkey, gruyere, and baby greens.

• Instead of cutting your granddaughter's grilled cheese in half, why not use a heart-shaped cookie cutter to remind her how much she's loved? This simple act can transform even the most mundane grilled cheese lunch into a memorable moment.

MARVELOUS MAC AND CHEESE

• Boil the macaroni from one box of store-bought mac and cheese. Mix the packet of dry cheese sauce with 1 C of premade pumpkin or butternut squash soup. Mix with cooked, drained macaroni. Put in a casserole dish and top with grated cheese. Broil for 8 minutes.

• Some browned ground beef, finely chopped red onion, and a can of kidney beans can transform a box of mac and cheese into chili mac. Top with sour cream and serve with corn chips. Or open a snack-size bag of corn chips and pour the chili mac right into the bag! Serve with a fork—and plenty of napkins.

• Stir ½ packet of taco seasoning and some fresh chopped tomatoes into your mac and cheese to add a bit of Mexican flair. Serve with tortilla chips.

• Add a can of tuna and some green peas to bump up the protein in your box of mac and cheese.

• If your granddaughter doesn't shy away from things that are green, cut up some steamed broccoli, cubes of ham and extra handful of grated cheddar cheese. You may want to add a bit more milk to help integrate all of the additional ingredients a little better.

• Add a few Tbsp. of softened cream cheese, leftover chicken, and just a drop of hot sauce for extra zing.

• If you really want to get fancy, in a kid-friendly way, roll small balls of your prepared mac and cheese in bread crumbs or panko and then deep fry them until they're lightly browned. Use toothpicks to serve your mac and cheese ball appetizers.

CHEF FOR A DAY

Help your granddaughter gain a better understanding of what it takes to plan, purchase, prepare, and clean up after a meal by declaring her Chef for a Day. Let her plan the menu by looking through cookbooks together. Talk about the importance of making a nutritious, as well as delicious, balanced meal, and the importance of considering how long different meals take to prepare.

Once you've decided on the menu, go grocery shopping together. Talk about how you choose ingredients, considering what's on sale, what you have coupons for, and what brands are her personal favorites—and why. Help your granddaughter figure out when she needs to begin preparing the meal, so it will be ready on time. When the time comes, help her set the table and prepare her chosen meal. Afterwards, help her clean up. Talk about what part of the process she liked best, what was her least favorite, and how successful she thought the meal was. If she enjoyed what she prepared, be sure and write out the recipe on a 3 x 5 card to take home.

To make the process more realistic—and more difficult—give your granddaughter a grocery budget she can't exceed or have her prepare a meal using only the ingredients you have on hand.

This may become one of your granddaughter's favorite activities at your house. If not, chances are she'll never complain about what you serve her for lunch again! Whatever the outcome, this is a great way to help your granddaughter gain the skills she'll need in the future. And while you're making meals together, you're also making memories.

CHEZ GRAND

If a love of cooking, or simply a love of food, is something you and your granddaughter share, let that love lead you in exciting new directions.

• Choose a food that you both love and perfect your own "secret" recipe. Give your dish a new twist by adding an unexpected spice, extract, or surprise ingredient. Brainstorm ideas with your granddaughter. Then, experiment with different texture and taste profiles. For instance, jazz up your standard chicken salad by topping it with a handful of crushed potato chips and some grated cheddar cheese. Bake for 20 minutes at 350°, and then serve in pita bread pockets. Or add a dash of chili powder to your chocolate chip cookies for an unexpected kick. Substitute orange juice for water in a boxed muffin recipe. Incorporate a variety of fruits and veggies into bottled salsa to make your own Grand variety. Every experiment may not be an absolute success, but you'll have fun trying and may come up with a new family favorite.

• Watch a cooking show together and then try one of the challenges for yourself. For example, try and make a sweet dessert that looks like a savory taco or master a tricky recipe, like French macarons.

• Work with your granddaughter to come up with your own restaurant or food truck concept. Come up with a fun theme and name. Create a menu. Design what your official outdoor sign would look like. You may even want to try and cook what you think would be the specialty dish you'd be known for.

inch worms

To make this cute little inch worm together with your grand-daughter you will need:

- Celery
- Cream cheese
- Cherry tomatoes, grapes, or olives
- Peppercorns
- Toothpicks

On a piece of celery, put 5-7 cherry tomatoes, grapes, or olives. Use small pieces of toothpicks to hold them together.

Make eyes with two dabs of cream cheese and two peppercorns. Cut a toothpick in half to form antennae…how cute they are!

ALIEN APPLES

- Green apple
- Blueberries
- Grapes
- Cloves
- Frosting Tube
- Toothpicks

Cut chunks of apple to create the shape of an alien.
Toothpicks topped with blueberries make antennae.
Add cloves to grapes for eyes, and attach with toothpicks.
Draw a mouth with frosting tube.

EDIBLE SCULPTURE

When snack time comes around, why not make artwork you can eat? Simply combine 1 C sunflower seed butter, 1 C of corn syrup, 1¼ C nonfat dry milk, and 1¼ C confectioner's sugar. Next, use the clay to make small sculptures that you can paint with food color. (You may want to use disposable gloves to minimize the mess.) Use them as cupcake toppers or as an edible decoration on a lunch plate. They're as much fun to create as they are to eat!

CRAZY QUILT CAKE

Instead of making individual cupcakes, bake a sheet cake with your granddaughter's help. Allow it to cool. Then cut it into 24 squares. Each of you take one dozen squares and decorate as you wish! Set out a variety of toppings and decorations. Here are a few ideas: tubes or tubs of frosting, lemon curd, sprinkles, small candies, skinny licorice ropes, raisins, nuts, sanding sugar, etc. Get creative in your decorating! Make each piece a miniature work of art. Then, put all of the pieces back into the 9 x 13 cake pan. Share it with the rest of the family!

DEVILED EGG CHICKS

Grandma, make your favorite deviled egg recipe, only instead of slicing the eggs in half lengthwise, cut off the top (about 1/3 of the egg). Stuff the yolk mixture in the bottom half, allowing it to overflow over the top. Set the stuffed egg in an egg cup or make small lettuce nests to keep eggs upright. To make your chick's face, use small pieces of black olive as eyes and a small triangle from a carrot slice for a beak. Put the top of the boiled egg white on top of the yolk face. Almost too cute to eat!

HOLIDAY TREATS

HATS OFF TO SANTA

Purchase store-bought brownie bites, white pre-made frosting (or canned whipped cream), fresh strawberries, and white chocolate chips. Cut the stem and top from the strawberries. Pipe the frosting or whipped cream in a circle near the edge of the brownie bites. Place a strawberry, cut side down, on each brownie bite. Pipe a small dot of frosting or whipped cream on the top of each strawberry. Place a white chocolate chip on top. Instant Santa hat!

HOLIDAY HOUSES

When you don't have the time, energy, or interest in creating a gingerbread house, try this easy holiday alternative. Cut a store-bought frozen pound cake (still frozen) into 8, 1" slices. Trim each slice to resemble the front of a house with a pointed, or slanted, roof. Microwave canned icing at 50% power for about 30 seconds, until it is warmed through. Pour the warm icing into a shallow dish. Stick a fork in the bottom of each house façade and dip it into the icing, keeping the bottom unfrosted. Keeping the fork in place, set the frosted façades on a cookie sheet. (The curved fork tines will keep the houses suspended while they dry and also makes a great handle to hold onto while decorating.) Using small dabs of icing, attach candies and sprinkles to finish decorating your houses. When they are finished, you can stand them up to create a cozy village you can eat.

SWEET HOLIDAY HUMMUS

Blend 1 15 oz. can of chickpeas (drained and rinsed), 1 15 oz. can of pumpkin puree, and ½ C sunflower butter in a food processor or blender. Slowly add ½ C maple syrup. Add 2 tsp. each of cinnamon, nutmeg, and vanilla extract and blend until smooth. Scoop mixture into a bowl. Top with pumpkin seeds and a sprinkle of cinnamon and serve with cinnamon-sugar pita chips.

HOT COCOA FLOAT

When you're craving a bit of summer in the dead of winter, here's a treat you and your granddaughter can make in a jiffy. Grate 1 oz. of bittersweet chocolate into a large mug. Pour hot milk over the chocolate and stir until it is completely blended. Using a cookie scoop, but a small scoop of ice cream on top. Add whipped cream and a sprinkle of grated chocolate or crushed candy canes on top, if you so desire!

CHEESY STARS

Using a star-shaped cookie cutter, cut stars out of ½" thick slices of sourdough bread. Place on an ungreased cookie sheet. Spread 1 tsp. of store-bought pesto (or cream cheese, a soft herbed cheese spread, or mayo, for granddaughters with a less exotic palate) on top of each slice. Cut slices of cheese with star-shaped cookie cutter and place on the pesto-topped bread. Bake in a 375° oven for about 8 minutes or until the cheese is melted.

MARBLED EGGS

This is an easy, eggs-cellent treat that's sure to delight! Thaw a container of frozen whipped topping, and then swirl food coloring through to create a marbled design. Try green and yellow for Easter, red and green for Christmas, or the favorite colors of your special little one. Press unpeeled hard-boiled eggs halfway into the marbled mixture, allowing them to sit for 10 minutes. Turn them over, and let them sit in the mixture for another 10 minutes. Rinse with water. Allow them to dry on a cooling rack or paper towel. Now your colorful eggs are ready to peel and eat!

COLORFUL DEVILED EGGS

Beauty doesn't have to only be shell deep! It's easy to add a bit of playful pizzazz to your favorite deviled egg recipe. Peel cooled hard-boiled eggs and cut them in half, setting the hard-boiled yolks aside in a separate bowl. Add a few drops of food coloring to a pot of water and soak the egg halves for several minutes, until the white has achieved the desired color. Prepare the filling, stuff, and serve.

Making Traditions & Treasures

For memorable times together, share your stories, photographs, and dreams...
then make new memories as you create special one-of-kind treasures to keep.

INSPIRE ME

**Posters sporting motivational sayings or inspiring quotes are a
popular choice for bedroom décor for countless young girls. Work
with your granddaughter to turn her favorite quotes—or her own
words of wisdom—into posters for her room. Cut letters from
magazines or use a calligraphy pen to write your granddaughter's
chosen message on poster board. Then have her decorate the rest
of the board with her own artwork or a photo collage. Use this same
idea to make greeting cards for friends out of cardstock, discussing
what message your granddaughter would like to convey. Then, work
together on the best way to capture this in words, pictures, glitter,
stickers...whatever fits the mood of her chosen message best.**

FAMILY FAVORITES COOKBOOK

It's great to teach your granddaughter how to make some "family
favorites," recipes that her Mom or Dad enjoyed when they were
her age. But take your cooking lesson a step further by creating
a family cookbook. Take photos of you and your granddaughter
creating your favorite recipes together. Then, create an online photo
album that includes the pictures and the recipes. This will become a
keepsake she can treasure, and use, for years to come. One day, she
may even share it with her own grandchildren, passing down what
you've taught her.

SWIRLY CURLY BUTTERFLIES

Paper towel or toilet paper cores are excellent for this project. Or make tubes out of construction paper or light-weight cardboard. Along with scissors, glue, crayons or markers, and maybe glitter pens and pipe cleaners, you're all set to create swirly curly butterflies.

Cut a tube into 1/2" circles.

For the wings, pinch one end of four circles and glue them together.

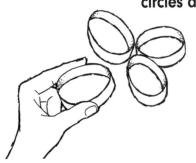

For the antennae, cut two circles open. Wind one end of each strip around a pencil to form a curl, and then attach to the four circles, as shown. Add a body by attaching a short piece of pipe cleaner, or a small strip of black paper.

Create a wall hanging by adding your butterflies to a stem made out of circles and a few strips curled at the end. Arrange, embellish, and decorate as desired!

FOIL-EMBOSSED FUN

Whether it's a welcome sign, a holiday message, or original artwork, foil-embossing adds an upscale twist on a Grandma/Granddaughter art project. You will need a piece of cardboard (even the front or back of a cereal box will do), heavy-duty foil, yarn, glue, a paint brush, and child-safe permanent markers. Glue pieces of yarn on the cardboard to create words or the outline of your chosen design. Cut a piece of foil about 2" larger in size than your cardboard. Use a small paintbrush to spread a light layer of glue all over the non-shiny side of the foil. Carefully center the cardboard (design-side down) over the glue-covered foil. Fold the excess foil over the edges, gluing them in place. Flip the cardboard over, design-side up. Starting in the middle and working toward the edge, use the pointed end of the paintbrush to carefully smooth the foil over the cardboard, helping to pull it taut over the yarn design. You can either leave your sign or design as is or color the area in between the raised yarn areas with markers to make an eye-catching work of art.

PHOTO BOMB ART

With your granddaughter, look through any duplicate or "reject" photos you may have that are gathering dust around your home. Cut out faces, trees, pets...anything that appeals to you to use to make a personalized collage. Then, draw a picture, gluing the images cut from your photos onto the artwork. It might be fun to give your granddaughter a picture of you—and you use one of her—that you incorporate into a picture. With a bit of imagination and a few crayons or markers, you can turn your granddaughter into a superhero or have her turn you into a dinosaur!

A TEA-RIFFIC TRADITION

A cup of tea is more than a beverage. It's an invitation to conversation! There are so many different ways to celebrate the gift of your granddaughter in a tea party setting. Choose which ideas work best for her age and interests—and then turn your Tea Time into a timeless tradition you continue to share as the years go by.

- Dress for the occasion. Let your granddaughter choose an outfit from your closet, complete with jewelry, and a hat or scarf. Add a touch of make-up to make the occasion feel extra special and grown-up.

- Fashion your own British fascinators out of a hairband or a paper plate tied in place with a ribbon. Add curled ribbons, plastic or crepe paper flowers, shapes cut from construction paper...use your imagination and whatever you happen to have on hand.

- Branch out from the kitchen or dining room for your Tea Time. Have a picnic outside if the weather is nice or pitch an indoor tent and pretend you're dining in the wild.

- Offer different sweeteners for your granddaughter to try with her tea, such as flavored honeys or jams. Or add a dash of lemonade to her cup for a bit of extra zing.

- Cut finger sandwiches into fun shapes with cookie cutters. Try raisin bread with apple butter, egg salad with pickles, or cucumber and cream cheese.

- Splurge for a birthday or special occasion by taking your granddaughter for Tea Time at a British or Japanese tea house. Keep your pinkies up and practice your poshest manners.

TEA TIME ENTERTAINMENT

Add a bit of imaginative play to your Tea Time to make it especially memorable. Here are a few ideas to jump start a few Tea-riffic traditions.

- Try speaking with a British accent throughout your Tea Time.

- Take on a different persona for your Tea Time. Choose a fancy name, like Lady Earl Goodly Grey or the Duchess of Sippingly. Try to stay in character, both you and your granddaughter, and carry on a conversation about your imaginary life.

- Visit an antique shop and each pick out a special tea cup and saucer. Use this every time you enjoy Tea Time together.

- After Tea Time, watch a British movie with your granddaughter and talk about how your lives are similar, and how they differ, from the main characters.

- Stack sugar cubes. Compete to see how high you can stack them before they tip over.

- Use sugar cubes to build a British castle or humble country village.

- Try the Sugar Cube Shuffle. Stack 3 sugar cubes in a teaspoon and then race across the room to deposit them into a tea cup—without dropping them along the way.

- Remove the lid from a tea pot and try tossing unused tea bags into the opening.

- Play Tea-Tac-Toe. Make a 3 by 3 grid out of masking tape on the floor. Toss unused tea bags, trying to score three in a row.

Tongue Twisters to Try

Can a clam cram in a clean cream can?

Roberta ran rings 'round the Roman ruins.

Wayne went to Wales to watch walruses.

Sheila shines shoes in a shoeshine shop.

If a dog chews shoes, whose shoes does he choose to chew?

I thought a thought,
but the thought I thought wasn't the thought
you thought I thought.

Six slippery, slimy snails slide slowly seaward.

Peter Piper picked a peck of pickled peppers.
A peck of pickled peppers Peter Piper picked.
If Peter Piper picked a peck of pickled peppers,
where's the peck of pickled peppers Peter Piper picked?

Swan swam over the sea –
swim, swan, swim!
Swan swam back again – well swum, swan!

How many yaks could a yak pack pack,
if yak packs could pack yaks?

POLKA DOT JEWELRY

With a bit of patience and a steady hand, you and your granddaughter can create polka dot pendants you'll be proud to wear or give away as gifts. Cut a piece of matboard into your desired shape, such as a heart, circle, butterfly, etc. Punch a hole through it (which you will use to hang the pendant) with a sturdy hole punch or small screwdriver. (Grandma, this will be your job!) Gather a variety of "paintbrushes," such as cotton swabs, toothpicks, and finely sharpened pencils. Then, using acrylic paints, create a scene using dots of different sizes, courtesy of your unconventional paintbrushes. You may want to try out your idea on a piece of paper first, and then recreate it on your matboard pendant. Finish your pendant by threading it on a lanyard, piece of cord, leather, string, or colorful gift wrap twine.

FLIP-TOP LOCKETS

Here's a hand-held trinket that's quick and easy to make. Clean a used, plastic flip-top cap. Ones used for squirt bottles of condiments or salad dressing work well. Find a small photo of your face (or anyone else who your granddaughter knows will always love her, no matter what). Using the cap as a template, cut the photo so it fits inside. Secure it by putting a piece of double-sided tape on the back. Write a word of encouragement on a 3 x 5 card that fits into the same-sized small circle. Cut it out and place it on the other side on the inside of the cap. Then, when your granddaughter needs a bit of encouragement, she can flip the cap open and shut, and see your smiling face and read your heartfelt message.

PERSONALIZED JOURNAL

Add a little bit of love to a blank journal or sketchbook by doing a Grandma to Granddaughter trade. Write a heartfelt message to your granddaughter, draw a picture, or write a poem about her, on the cover or first inside page of a blank journal or sketchbook. Have her do the same for you. Then, trade blank books—and fill them up with whatever suits your fancy. Every time you use them, you'll both be reminded of your special relationship.

EVERYTHING OLD IS NEW

Using an old book you no longer need, challenge your granddaughter (and yourself!) to write a brand new story. Using words cut from the pages of the used book, glue them onto a page of paper, to create a new story. Read your stories aloud to each other. Don't forget to add an intriguing title.

GRAND GREETINGS

As our granddaughters get older, they may not always appreciate a show of affection in public. Work out a special "I love you" gesture or secret message that only you and your granddaughter share. For instance, instead of holding her hand, give her thumb a squeeze. Put her hair behind one ear. Give her a private wink. Share silly faces when no one else is looking. Or agree that every time you say, "I really love ice cream" (or some other chosen phrase) that what you're really expressing is how much you love each other. The key is to make your secret message or gesture a tradition, repeating it every time you see one another.

WONDERFUL WOMEN

Help your granddaughter (and yourself!) gain an appreciation for how women who have come before you have affected your own life by doing a little historical research. Choose an area of interest, such as medicine, space travel, literature, conservation, architecture, civil rights, education, zoology, etc. If your granddaughter has a specific career in mind that she hopes to pursue one day, why not start with that field?

Then, search the internet for women who have made noteworthy contributions to your chosen field. Together, choose one individual to focus on. Check out books from the library and do internet searches together to find out everything you can about her. Put together a short biography of her life. Draw pictures of her. Write— or simply talk—about how her life has affected your own and how what she has done is an inspiration to you. Then talk about how you hope your own lives will affect future generations of women in a positive way.

If you need a little help choosing a remarkable woman, here are a few names to begin your search: Malala Yousafzai (Pakistani educational activist, youngest person to win the Nobel Peace Prize), Sojourner Truth (American abolitionist and women's rights activist), Mae Jemison (engineer and physician, the first African American woman to travel to space), Ada Lovelace (English mathematician and writer who helped program the first computers), Mabel Ping-Hua Lee (advocate for women's rights at the age of 16 and became the first Chinese woman to earn a PhD in Economics), Zaha Hadid (award winning Iraqi-born British architect), Amelia Earhart (pioneer in American aviation), and Marie-Louise Bottineau-Baldwin (Chippewa Native American attorney and civil rights activist).

POCKET-SIZED SURPRISE

Family traditions need not be grand gestures. They can be as simple as putting a piece of candy in your pocket. To turn this simple act into a relational building block, choose an item of clothing you wear relatively frequently that has a pocket. Then, every time you wear it in your granddaughter's presence, be sure there's a special treat hidden inside. Don't wear it too frequently, just often enough that your granddaughter recognizes it, and knows a little surprise is headed her way.

SPEAK HER LANGUAGE

If your granddaughter has a phone, ask her for permission to text now and then. (Don't overdo it. Once a week is plenty!) Keep it short and sweet, a "Miss you!" or "Thinking of you!" with a fun emoji is sufficient. Send a word of encouragement on days when she has a big test or sporting event. Mix it up by sending a fun photo of your pet, a thoughtful or funny meme, or one of the jokes in this book. If your granddaughter texts you back, resist the temptation to begin a long conversation—unless she is the one asking you questions. If she doesn't respond, don't take it as rejection. Not every text requires a response. Just let your granddaughter know that she's on your mind and in your heart.

DESIGN DOODLERS

Bring out the cookie cutters! But instead of baking, use them as templates for doodle creations. Using a fine point marker, trace around the exterior of the cookie cutter. Then, begin filling the inside with doodle designs. Doodling is the perfect backdrop to conversation, so doodle along with your granddaughter, while chatting about anything and everything that comes to mind.

TREASURED TOUCHSTONES

A touchstone may be a personal symbol or emblem that represents your dream and that helps you to stay on track.

Stay closely connected to your granddaughter, even when you're apart, by creating a shared touchstone. These touchstones should be small, something that can be carried in your pocket, purse, or backpack, or simply set someplace where you will see them every day, such as your nightstand. The key is, every time you catch sight of this item, or touch it in your purse or backpack, you think of the other person—and send a little loving thought or prayer her way.

Your touchstone can be a found item. For instance, you can each pick up a small shell when you're at the beach together and exchange them, keeping them close until you see each other again. Or, you can pick up stones together on a walk through a park. Then, with paint or a permanent marker, write a word or brief note on the stone. For instance, "You are beautiful!" or "I'm so proud of you!"

You can also use your imagination to create your own meaningful touchstone. If you both love root beer, why not use a bottle cap as a touchstone? Cut out a circle from a 3 x 5 card that fits inside the bottle cap. Draw a picture or write a message with a fine point marker.

If you enjoy baking together, write messages to each other on the bowl of a wooden spoon and hang it in the kitchen. If you both enjoy reading, make bookmarks for each other out of cardstock. Brainstorm together to come up with the perfect touchstone that not only symbolizes your relationship, but that will remind you of how fortunate you are to have each other.

HAPPY ENDINGS

It's been said that all good things must come to an end, and unfortunately, that's true of visits with our granddaughters. But, instead of focusing on saying good-bye, let's focus on the wonderful time we've shared and talk about what we'd like to do the next time we get together.

A memorable way to end your visit with your granddaughter is to give her a little gift right before she leaves, something she can open on her way home. It could be a sweet treat to eat, a photo from your time together, a craft she can do on her own, or a note that reminds her how much you love her and look forward to getting to know her better in the years to come.

Remember, time apart is an opportunity to continue to mature in new and interesting ways. The more content we are with who we are, the better friends and grandmothers we'll become. Let's keep exploring, learning, and growing, regardless of how old or young we happen to be.